BEFORE YOU SAY
"I DO"®

H. NORMAN WRIGHT
& WES ROBERTS

HARVEST HOUSE PUBLISHERS

EUGENE, OREGON

Unless otherwise indicated all Scripture quotations in this book are taken from the King James Version of the Bible.

Verses marked AMP are taken from The Amplified Bible, Old Testament, Copyright © 1965 and 1987 by The Zondervan Corporation, and from The Amplified New Testament, Copyright © 1954, 1958, 1987 by The Lockman Foundation. Used by permission. (www.Lockman.org)

Verses marked NASB are taken from the New American Standard Bible, © 1960, 1962, 1963, 1968, 1971, 1972, 1973, 1975, 1977 by The Lockman Foundation. Used by permission. (www.Lockman.org)

Verses marked TLB are taken from The Living Bible, Copyright © 1971 owned by assignment by Illinois Regional Bank N.A. (as trustee). Used by permission of Tyndale House Publishers, Inc., Carol Stream, Illinois 60188. All rights reserved.

Cover © photo rasstock / Fotolia

Cover design by Writely Designed, Enumclaw, Washington

BEFORE YOU SAY "I DO" is a registered trademark of The Hawkins Children's LLC. Harvest House Publishers, Inc., is the exclusive licensee of the federally registered trademark BEFORE YOU SAY "I DO."

BEFORE YOU SAY "I DO" ®
Copyright © 1977, 1997 by Harvest House Publishers
Published 2015 by Harvest House Publishers
Eugene, Oregon 97402
www.harvesthousepublishers.com

ISBN 978-0-7369-6110-3 (pbk.)
ISBN 978-0-7369-6111-0 (eBook)

Printed in the United States of America

16 17 18 19 20 21 22 23 / VP-CD / 10 9 8 7 6 5 4 3

Contents

꩜

CHAPTER 1

What Is Marriage?

ॐ

You are probably about to begin one of the most important stages of your life—marriage. Marriage contains unique and interesting potential. As one bright optimist put it, "Marriage is the only game of chance in town where both players can win or both lose!" This manual has been developed to help you decrease the risk element from marriage. We trust that as you and your fiancé work through this program, your present relationship will be strengthened and enhanced as a prelude to an enriching, fulfilling, and growing marriage. We also hope that you will have a much more realistic perception of yourself, your fiancé, and your upcoming marriage.

1. Define marriage. What is its purpose?

2. Do you believe that marriage is a contract? Why or why not?

3. How do you think your fiancé will answer these questions?

4. Read the following quotations. After you have read each of them indicate which portions you agree with and which portions you disagree with.

"Marriage resembles a pair of shears, so joined that they cannot be separated; often moving in opposite directions, yet always punishing anyone who comes between them."[1]

"Is marriage a private action of two persons in love, or a public act of two pledging a contract? Neither, it is something other. Very much other! Basically, the Christian view of marriage is not that it is primarily or essentially a binding legal and social contract. The Christian understands marriage as a covenant made under God and in the presence of fellow members of the Christian family. Such a pledge endures, not because of the force of law or the fear of its actions, but because an unconditional covenant has been made. A covenant more solemn, more binding, more permanent than any legal contract."[2]

"A system by means of which persons who are sinful and contentious are so caught up by a dream and a purpose bigger than themselves that they work through the years, in spite of repeated disappointment, to make the dream come true."[3]

"Marriage is a relationship between man and woman intended by God to be a monogamous relationship, intended to be a permanent bond in which many needs are satisfied—the need to love and be loved, the need for deep friendship, for sharing, for companionship, for sexual satisfaction, for children, the need to escape loneliness. Marriage ought to be a bond of love, reflecting the love Christ has for His people, a bond of sacrificial love where husband and wife have become one, one flesh, a unity."[4]

Read Genesis 2:18-25

1. Who originated the marriage institution?

2. What are the purposes of marriage, and why was it originated? (See Genesis 1:28; 2:18; Ephesians 5:22-32.)

   (1)

   (2)

   (3)

   (4)

3. How is marriage good? (Genesis 2:18; Hebrews 13:4.)

4. What is a *helper*, in your opinion? In your fiancé's opinion?

5. What does "leaving mother and father" involve?

6. What do the words "shall cleave" or "will be united" mean?

7. What do the words "be one flesh" mean to you?

8. List six ways that you can promote and maintain the oneness characteristic in your upcoming marriage.

   (1)

   (2)

   (3)

   (4)

   (5)

   (6)

9. List three of the most important Scripture verses upon which you would like to base your marriage relationship. (Please use passages other than Ephesians 5:21-33; 1 Corinthians 13; and 1 Peter 3:1-7, as most couples automatically look to these. They are important, but think through other important passages that will assist you in establishing the type of marriage you are seeking.)

(1)

(2)

(3)

Here is another definition of marriage that you may want to consider. "The marriage relationship is a school, a learning and growing environment in which (if everything is as it should be) both partners can grow and develop. The relationship grows along with them. If you can see marriage as an opportunity for growth, you can be satisfied and can satisfy your spouse."

Dr. David Hubbard graphically described the marriage relationship when he said, "Marriage does not demand perfection. But it must be given priority. It is an institution for sinners. No one else need apply. But it finds its finest glory when sinners see it as God's way of leading us through his ultimate curriculum of love and righteousness."[5] Have you ever thought about the purpose of marriage in that light?

Here's another definition of marriage. Consider it carefully, and then talk over your feelings with your partner: "A Christian marriage is a total commitment of two people to the person of Jesus Christ and to each other. It is a commitment in which nothing is held back. Marriage is a pledge of mutual fidelity; it is a partnership of mutual subordination. A Christian marriage is similar to a solvent, a freeing up of the man and woman to be themselves and become all that God intends for them to become. Marriage is a refining process that God will use to have us become the man or woman He wants us to become. Think about it. God will use your marriage for His purpose. He will mold and refine you for your own benefit and for His glory."

You may be thinking that when you marry there will be two individuals involved in that marriage. That is true, but there is a third party who can give an even greater meaning to your individual and married life—that person is Jesus Christ. In what way will the presence of Jesus Christ in your life make a difference in your marriage?

Read Matthew 7:24-27. This passage is talking about building your house upon a firm foundation. List what you believe are ten firm foundations which will go into making a solid marriage relationship.

1.

2.

3.

4.

5.

6.

7.

8.

9.

10.

Reasons for Marriage

There are many reasons and motivating factors for marriage. What are yours? Have you ever thought about them? Respond to the following and discuss your answers with your fiancé.

1. What will you receive out of marriage that you wouldn't receive by remaining single?

2. On a separate piece of paper, list the reasons why you are marrying your fiancé. After you have done that, list the reasons why you think your fiancé is marrying you. Then share the results.

Now compare your reasons for marriage with the following list, which has been compiled by several specialists in marriage and family life education. These are unhealthy reasons for marriage. If you find that any of these appear either on your list or in your mind, you should spend time discussing them with your fiancé and your marriage advisor.

1. To spite or get back at your parents.

2. Because of a negative self-image—marrying your fiancé will make you feel worthwhile and will give meaning to your life.

3. To be a therapist or counselor to your fiancé.

4. Fear of being left out—being single forever.

5. Fear of independence.

6. Marrying on the rebound—you were hurt in a former love relationship and to ease your hurt you immediately choose another.

7. Fear of hurting the other person—you're afraid of what will happen to your fiancé if you break up even though you know that marriage is not the answer.

8. To escape an unhappy home.

9. Because you are pregnant or your fiancé is pregnant.

10. Because you have had sex.

A few of the positive reasons for marriage include:

1. Companionship.

2. To work together and fulfill your own and your future mate's needs.

3. To fulfill sexual needs in the way God intends.

4. Love (an adequate blending of the various types of love, as explained in Chapter 3).

5. Because you are convinced that it is God's will for you to marry this person.

Evaluate your "marriageability" by examining the personality traits of yourself and your fiancé. List eight character or personality traits that you feel would help a marriage.

1.

2.

3.

4.

5.

6.

7.

8.

Turn in your Bible to Galatians 5:22,23 and read over the fruit of the Spirit. Would these traits, manifested in a person, increase the potential of success in marriage?

If so, indicate which of these you manifest and which of them you are still having difficulty displaying.

In addition to using the fruit of the Spirit as a guide for evaluating the potential success of a marriage, consider these eight marriageability traits that give a person a greater possibility of having an enriched and satisfying marriage.

1. Adaptability and flexibility—the ability to change and adapt.

2. Empathy—the ability to be sensitive to the needs, hurts, and desires of others, to feel with them and experience the world from their perspective.

3. The ability to work through problems.

4. The ability to give and receive love.

5. Emotional stability—accepting and controlling one's emotions.

6. Communication skills.

7. Similarities between the two people.

8. Similar family background.

The natural inclination is to look at this list and say, "Oh yes, that's us. We are like that and have these characteristics." If you feel these traits are present in your relationship, give a specific example of how each of the first six traits was manifested in the past two weeks. Then, for traits seven and eight, give examples of each type of similarity.

1.

2.

3.

4.

5.

6.

7.   (1)

   (2)

   (3)

   (4)

   (5)

8.   (1)

   (2)

   (3)

   (4)

   (5)

Now that you've taken a close look at the fundamental issues of marriage, it's natural to move to organizing and implementing the details of your wedding day. "Planning Your Wedding Together" on page 87 will help both of you make this a special, unifying time of preparation.

CHAPTER 2

Uniqueness and Acceptance in Marriage

~~~

Your partner is not you. He or she is "other," created in God's image, not yours. He or she has a right to be other, to be treated and respected as other.

Differences. How do you learn to adjust to the differences in your partner without losing who you are? How do you learn to appreciate another person's uniqueness? How can you learn to live with this person who is so different from you?

"When you marry, do you end up marrying someone who is your opposite or someone who is similar?" The answer is "yes." It's both. There will be similarities as well as differences, and you have to learn to adjust to both. Think of it like this:

> We marry for our similarities. We stay together for our differences.
> Similarities satiate; differences attract.
> Differences are rarely the cause of conflict in marriage; the problems arise from our similarities. Differences are the occasion, similarities are the cause.
> The differences may serve as the triggering event, as the issue for debate, but our similarities create the conflict between us.
> The very same differences that initially drew

us together later pull us apart and still later may draw us near again. Differences first attract, then irritate, then frustrate, then illuminate and finally may unite us. Those traits that intrigue in courtship, amuse in early marriage, begin to chafe in time and infuriate in conflicts of middle marriages; but maturation begins to change their meaning and the uniqueness of the other person becomes prized, even in the very differences that were primary irritants.[6]

Differences abound in marriage. Generally, they can be divided into two types. The first includes those that can't be changed, such as age, race, looks, home, and cultural background. Your personal body metabolism will affect where you want the temperature in the home, whether you wake up bright and eager, ready to face the day, or whether you need an hour to get both eyes focusing. These characteristics cannot be changed.

But the other category includes those differences that can be changed: personal habits in the bathroom or at the dinner table, whether you like to get up early and your spouse enjoys sleeping late, or whether one likes going out three nights a week and the other prefers watching television at home.

Think about this: "If you plan to marry, it is certain that you have a preconceived fantasy of your ideal mate or the perfect marriage. After a while you will begin to realize that your fantasy and the person you have married will begin to diverge sharply. At that point you may embark upon a reform program, forgetting that only God can make a tree. You misconstrued the words of the wedding ceremony 'and the two shall become one' to mean that your mate should become like you and your fantasy. You want to become one in likes, preferences, interests, hobbies, ideas, even reactions and feelings: *Yours!* The oneness in marriage is not similarity or sameness in matters relating to ideas or feelings but oneness in understanding. Any attempt to mold our mates in an effort to match them to our fantasies is arrogance on our part and an insult to them. While it is true that we can never mold or remake another person, we can 'allow' him [or her] to change."[7]

The instruction on right living in Ephesians 4:2 can be applied to the marriage relationship. "Living as becomes you—with complete lowliness of mind (humility) and meekness (unselfishness, gentleness, mildness), with patience, bearing with one another and making allowances because you love one another" (AMP).

Look at the last part of the verse: "making allowances because you love one another." List six specific examples of how this portion can be applied in your future marriage relationship. Try to think of these in relation to your differentness.

1.

2.

3.

4.

5.

6.

Similarities	Differences	Effect
How are my fiancé and I similar?	How are my fiancé and I different?	How can these differences and similarities complement one another in our marriage?
		Which of the differences have you thanked God for?

Differences in Marriage—
The Potential for Growth
and Enhancement

Yes, every person who marries has characteristics similar to the one he or she marries. But he or she also has many that are different. Different ways of perceiving, thinking, feeling, and behaving are part of marital adjustment. Differentness is important because it holds out the promise of need fulfillment for each person.

It is important to remember that one of the main motivating factors toward marriage is the need to feel complete because of what the other person has to offer. Consciously or unconsciously people choose others who can help them feel complete.

On one hand, this innate differentness contains the seeds for hurt and disruption. Why? The answer is quite simple. We are threatened by the differences in our spouse. We are afraid that we might have to adjust our way of thinking and doing things. We also may believe that "if it's different, it's wrong."

Many problems occur because of the lack of tolerance for differences of attitude or opinions in the marital relationship. You will be vaguely aware of differences when you marry. You probably don't say now that your partner is different—more likely "unique." But after a while you will say . . . different. At first you may try to *accommodate*. You tolerate, overlook, or deny differences to avoid conflict. Then you may try to *eliminate* the differences by demanding, pressuring, or manipulating your spouse.

But eventually you will learn to *appreciate* the differences because you discover that they are necessary and indispensable. And because of this, you will be able to *celebrate* them. You'll delight in them. You'll welcome them. You'll encourage their growth. As you go through this process, you will discover that you didn't marry the wrong person.[8]

Consider these thoughts: "In the midst of the marital struggle the honeymoon dream vanishes, and the despair over the old relationship comes up for reexamination. Suddenly each spouse turns his eyes away from the partner, and looks inwardly and asks, 'What am I doing to my partner? What is wrong with me? What am I misunderstanding? What must I do to rescue this marriage?'

"If honestly asked, the answers are not far behind: 'I really married my wife because of her difference. It is not my job to make her over, but rather to discover and to value that difference. But before I can do that I must accept my difference, and I really need her to help me discover my uniqueness. My task is not to mold her into a beautiful vase, but to participate with her to discover that beautiful vase even as we discover it in me.

"'How arrogant of me to think I could shape another human being! How humble it makes me to realize that I need to yield to another and thereby be changed! Our relationship will change both of us—in a process of being shaped into a form far more beautiful than either could imagine.'"[9]

"We try to change people to conform to our ideas of how they should be. So does God. But there the similarity ends. Our ideas of what the other person should do or how he should act may be an improvement or an imprisonment. We may be setting the other person free of behavior patterns that are restricting his development, or we may be simply chaining him up in another behavioral bondage."[10]

In reality, we marry the right person—far more right than we can know. In a mysterious, intuitive, perhaps instinctive fashion we are drawn by both similarities and differences, by needs and anxieties, by dreams and fears to choose our complement, our reflection in another.

We always marry the right person, and the discovery of that rightness moves us into the third marriage within a marriage. We at last begin to appreciate what we had sought to eliminate.

As we discover that we knew more than we knew when we chose whom we chose, appreciation begins to break into a gentle flame. In appreciation, we discover that people who marry each other reflect each other. There is a similar level of maturity, a parallel set of self-understandings and self-acceptance in most couples choosing each other. The two express their self-image and self-valuation in the person selected.

People who marry each other complete each other in a puzzling yet pronounced way. The missing is supplied, the imbalanced is brought into equilibrium, the dormant is enriched by what is dominant in the other.[11]

The adventure of marriage is discovering who your partner really is. The excitement is in finding out who your partner will become.

Family History and Interview Questions

(Adapted from *Finding Your Perfect Mate* by H. Norman Wright, Harvest House.)

Use the following questions to discover as much as you can about your partner.

- What special memories do you have about your childhood?

- How did you get along with each of your parents? What were they like? What did you like and dislike about your parents?

- What were your hurts and disappointments as a child?

- What were your hobbies and favorite games?

- How did you usually get into trouble?

- How did you usually try to get out of trouble?

- What did you enjoy about school activities?

- What pets did you have? Which were your favorites and why?

- What did you dream about doing when you were older?

- Did you like yourself as a child? Explain.

- Did you like yourself as a teenager? Explain.

- What were your talents and special abilities?

- What awards and achievements did you win?

- Did you have a nickname?

- Who were your close friends? Where are they today?

- Describe the area where you grew up—people, neighborhood, etc.

- What was your spiritual life like as a child? As an adolescent?

- Who were the Christians in your family?

- What were you afraid of? Do you have any of those fears today?

- How did you get along with your brothers and/or sisters? If you had none, which relatives were you closest to?

- What parts of your childhood would you like to relive? Why?

- What do you remember from your first day of school?

- Did you enjoy school? Why or why not? What was your favorite grade, and who were your favorite teachers?

- Who was your first date?

- Who were your other dates or boyfriends/girlfriends? What did you like and dislike about each one?

- Where did you go on dates?

- How did you feel when you liked someone and that person didn't care for you?

- How has being an adult changed your life?
- Compare yourself now to when you were 10.
- What have been your greatest disappointments? How have you handled them? What have you learned from them?
- At what age did you first like the opposite sex?
- What was your birth order in your family?
- Did you have enough money in your youth? Enough food and clothing?
- Who educated you in sex? What were your sexual experiences? What is your standard for sexual expression in your life now?
- What are your political views?
- What do you enjoy reading? Watching on TV?
- Have you ever had a child? Do you want children?
- What is your first memory?
- Who were your favorite relatives?
- Describe your education and job experiences. What were your emotional reactions to jobs, fellow employees, and bosses? What are your ambitions?
- What are your natural gifts? What do you consider your strong points? Weak points?
- What is your medical history?
- What is your favorite holiday, type of music, television program, and pastime?
- While growing up, did you think of marrying someday?
- Who are the five most important people in your life?
- Which Christian leaders or writers have influenced you?

- Where would you like to live? What country, state, city, house, and/or apartment?
- What are your views on aging?
- Describe the best year of your life.

Daily Log History Sheet

To assist you in becoming better acquainted with your potential partner, complete the following daily activity log with as much specific information as possible. It may be helpful to keep this with you at all times during a typical day. At the end of each hour, write down exactly what you did during that time. You will need to do this twice, once for a weekday and once for a day off.

1. When do you wake up?

2. When do you get up?

3. What steps do you take to get ready for the day? Example: Do you shower first or eat first? How much time do you need getting ready in the bathroom? How much time do you take preparing breakfast? Do you eat sitting down or on the run? Do you read the paper in the morning, have devotions, etc.? In other words, indicate your normal procedures and how much time you spend for each task.

4. As you drive to wherever you're going (work, school, etc.), do you enjoy the solitude or would you rather talk to someone? If you listen to the radio, what do you listen to?

5. Now that you've got the basic idea of what we're looking for, indicate what you do each hour of the day. Be sure to describe what you do on breaks, lunch, etc.

6. As you drive home, are you thinking about what went on during the day or what you're going to do in the evening? What do you enjoy doing for the first hour when you get home?

7. Describe in detail dinner preparations, what and where you like to eat, and what you do in the evening. When you get ready for bed, where do you put your clothes from this day? Do you prepare your clothes for the next day or wait until the morning? Do you go to sleep with the radio or TV on? Do you like it completely dark and quiet or do you leave a light on?

Please feel free to add any details or any pertinent information that will help your partner have a better idea of your daily lifestyle. Be sure you follow the same procedure for your day off, such as Saturday.

Once you have both completed these forms, share them with one another and discuss how being married will change your daily procedures.

Final questions

1. If you are bothered by the uniqueness of your fiancé, ask yourself, "What will it be like to be married to a person like me in so many ways? What will it be like being married to someone so different than I am? Will I like it?"

2. In what way will the presence of Jesus Christ in your life help you adjust to differences in your future marriage?

To assist you in fully discovering your uniqueness, as well as differences, ask your minister or counselor to administer the Myers Briggs Type Indicator (MBTI). You can save 20 years of frustration by discovering now how God uniquely created you and how you can learn to be compatible with your spouse. The MBTI helps you better understand your personality. It is the most accurate and insightful tool available to measure personality characteristics.

It is also important to expand your understanding by reading about who you are. A book designed to help you understand personality differences, gender differences, and learning style differences is *Communication: Key to Your Marriage* by H. Norman Wright.

CHAPTER 3

Love as a Basis for Marriage

❦

Most couples say they are marrying because they love their fiancé. Let's assume that in this society, in order to be married, you had to convince a jury in a court of law that you really did love the other person. Write in detail the facts you would present to a jury. Include in your presentation your own definition of love.

What is love? What does the world think love is? Here are several definitions. Which of these do you agree with?

"Love is a feeling you feel when you get a feeling that you've never felt before."

"Love is a perpetual state of anesthesia."

"Love is a find, a fire, a heaven, a hell—where pleasure, pain, and sad repentance dwell!"

"Love is a grave mental disease."

"To love somebody is not just a strong feeling—it is a decision, it is a judgment, it is a promise."

"Love is an unconditional commitment to an imperfect person."

The Biblical Concept of Love

What does the Word of God say about love?

Look up the following passages of Scripture to discover love from God's perspective. We suggest using a modern translation. What is the central thought or example in each passage?

1. Proverbs 17:17

2. Matthew 6:24

3. Matthew 22:37-39

4. Luke 6:27-35

5. Luke 10:25-37

6. John 3:16

7. John 13:34

8. Romans 13:8-10

9. Romans 14:15

10. 1 Corinthians 8:1

11. Galatians 2:20

12. Galatians 5:13

13. Galatians 6:2

14. Ephesians 4:2

15. Ephesians 5:2

16. Ephesians 5:25

17. Titus 2:3-5

18. 1 Peter 4:8

19. 1 John 3:16-18

First Corinthians 13:4-7 gives the Bible's definition of love. These verses indicate that love consists of many elements. As you consider them below, give three creative examples of how each could be applied in your marriage. Be specific.

1. Suffers long—endures offenses, is not hasty, waits for the Lord to right all wrongs.

(1)

(2)

(3)

2. Is kind—not inconsiderate, seeks to help, is constructive, blesses when cursed, helps when hurt, demonstrates tenderness.

(1)

(2)

(3)

3. Is not envious, but content—is not jealous of another person's success or competition.

(1)

(2)

(3)

4. Is not arrogant, but humble—not haughty, but lowly and gracious.

(1)

(2)

(3)

5. Is not boastful, but reserved—does not show off, try to impress, want to be the center of attraction.

(1)

(2)

(3)

6. Is not rude, but courteous.

(1)

(2)

(3)

7. Is not selfish, but self-forgetful.

(1)

(2)

(3)

8. Is not irritable, but good-tempered.

(1)

(2)

(3)

9. Is not vindictive or wrathful, but generous.

(1)

(2)

(3)

10. Does not delight in bringing another person's sins to light, but rejoices when another person obeys the truth.

(1)

(2)

(3)

11. Is not rebellious, but brave; is circumspect when it comes to another person's wrongdoing.

(1)

(2)

(3)

12. Is not suspicious, but trustful—not cynical, makes every allowance, looks for an explanation that will show the best in others.

(1)

(2)

(3)

13. Is not despondent, but hopeful—does not give up because it has been deceived or denied.

(1)

(2)

(3)

14. Is not conquerable, but invincible—can outlast problems.

(1)

(2)

(3)

A Love Problem?

After eight years of marriage Ken tells a marriage counselor that he no longer has any romantic feelings for his wife. "It isn't like when we were first married," he says. "I knew without a doubt I loved her then. I had strong emotional feelings that were unmistakable. Now that is all gone. I admire her. She is a wonderful woman, a good wife and mother. I'm really more attracted to a girl I used to date in high school."

Sandy is frustrated over the whole matter. She says she loves her husband and children and wants to hold her family together.

Neither wants a divorce. *"How can I regain that loving feeling for my wife?"* he asks. *"Was it something I did to destroy his love for me?"* she asks.

1. What are the causes of the problem?

   Sandy

   Ken

2. What should they do to resolve the problem?

   Sandy

   Ken

3. What suggestions does Revelation 2:1-5 give on how to fall in love again?

   (1)

   (2)

   (3)

Your Marriage Needs Three Types of Love—
Eros, Philia, Agape

Eros is the love that seeks sensual expression. Eros is romantic love, sexual love. It is inspired by the biological structure of human nature. The husband and wife, in a good marriage, will love each other romantically and erotically.

In a good marriage, the husband and wife are also friends. Friendship means companionship, communication, and cooperation. This is known as *philia*.

Agape is self-giving love, gift love, the love that goes on loving even when the other becomes unlovable. *Agape love is not just* something *that happens to you; it's something you* make *happen*. Love is a personal act of commitment. Christ's love (and hence the pattern for our love) is gift love. Christ's love for us is sacrificial love. Christ's love is unconditional. Christ's love is an eternal love. Agape is kindness. It is being sympathetic, thoughtful, and sensitive to the needs of your loved one. Agape is contentment. Agape love is forgiving love.

If individuals would put forth effort purposely to increase philia and agape love, all three types of love would increase. The friendship love of philia can enhance and enrich both of the others. The agape love, in turn, can increase and enhance the others. Both agape and philia can enrich the eros love so it does not diminish as much as it usually does. It too can flourish if properly nurtured, and, if so, the other types of love are reinforced. All three must be given conscious effort.

When you are married, what can you do to demonstrate these three kinds of love? Under each word on the next page, write five specific examples of what you will do to enhance your love relationship.

Eros	Philia	Agape
1.	1.	1.
2.	2.	2.
3.	3.	3.
4.	4.	4.
5.	5.	5.

What do you feel are the three main hindrances in marriage to developing love and continuing to grow?

1.

2.

3.

Your love will either live or die. What kills love? Love dies when you spend little or no time together and when you stop sharing activities that are mutually enjoyable.

Love is created or destroyed by failing to include pleasurable activities with your partner over a period of time.

Love dies from failure on the part of both individuals to reinforce appropriate behavior in each other. Smiling, caressing, complimenting, showing compassion, and spending time together are behaviors in marriage that must be reinforced. If they are not reinforced they may disappear. If your partner stops doing things that you like, your love feelings may disappear.

1. What do you do now to reinforce the behaviors that you enjoy?

2. What will you do when you are married?

3. How will the presence of Jesus Christ in your life help you to love your spouse through eros, philia, and agape love?

Something to Think About

Marital love requires the ability to put yourself in your partner's place, to understand that the differences that divide you are the differences of two unique personalities, rather than betrayals of your hopes and dreams. The unconditional willingness of each of you to understand and resolve these differences through the sharing of your deepest feelings, concerns, attitudes, and ideas is a fundamental component of marital love.

Postponement of your need for instant gratification when your partner feels no such need; sharing the struggle to triumph over adversities as well as sharing the joys and delights of being together; nurturing each other in defeat caused by forces beyond your control and renewing each other's courage to prevail in the face of despair; carrying necessary obligations and responsibilities as a flower rather than as a hundred-pound knapsack; acknowledging the everyday value of your partner in a look, a smile, a touch of the hand, a voiced appreciation of a meal or a new hairstyle, a spontaneous trip to a movie or a restaurant; trusting your partner always to be there when needed; knowing that he or she always has your best interests at heart even when criticism is given; loyalty and dedication to each other in the face of sacrifices that may have to be made.

All of these are additional components of marital love that courtship knows little about.[12]

CHAPTER 4

What Do You Expect from Marriage?

%^%

Every person who marries enters the marriage relationship with certain expectations. These expectations come from many sources, including parents, values, society, books, speakers, and our own ideas. It is important to take the time to find out what these expectations are, which can be achieved, which are realistic, and how to handle them when things do not go according to plans. The word *expectation* carries with it the attitude of hope. Hope has been defined as "the anticipation of something good." Hope is necessary, as it motivates us and keeps us going.

This next exercise will take some thought and time on your part. Write 20 expectations you will have of your fiancé when you are married. These can be simple or elaborate. For example, a husband might expect his wife to be at the door when he arrives home, always to be at home and never work, and to have sex with him whenever he wants it. A wife might expect her husband to go to her parents' house with her whenever she goes, to be the spiritual leader in their home, and to spend Saturdays at home and not out hunting.

List your expectations now, but do not discuss them with your fiancé yet.
(You will be using the columns on the right later.)

	C	S	N
1.			
2.			
3.			
4.			
5.			
6.			
7.			
8.			
9.			
10.			
11.			
12.			
13.			
14.			
15.			
16.			
17.			
18.			
19.			
20.			

Now list ten expectations you think your fiancé will have for you in marriage.

1.

2.

3.

4.

5.

6.

7.

8.

9.

10.

Let's briefly talk about disappointment. We all experience disappointments because some of our expectations, hopes, and dreams are not realized. List three of the most disappointing experiences of your life and then indicate how you handled the disappointment.

1.

2.

3.

Now let's go back to your 20 expectations of your future spouse. Take each expectation and, on a separate piece of paper, write one or two sentences indicating how your marriage relationship will be affected if this expectation was not met.

Now, take your list of 20 expectations and share your list with your fiancé. Take your fiancé's list and read it to yourself. As you read each one of your fiancé's expectations of you, place a check mark under the appropriate column. C stands for "cinch." You feel that the expectation you have just read is going to be a cinch to fulfill. S stands for "sweat." It will take some hard work and sweat, but it can be done. N stands for "no way." You feel that the expectation is impossible.

When the two of you have completed your evaluation of the expectations, give them back and then spend some time discussing them.

There are three very common expectations that couples have for their marriages. First, couples expect their marriages will work out and not end in divorce. This is an excellent goal, but what will be done to make it a reality? Write a paragraph indicating what you personally are bringing to this marriage that will make it work. When you and your fiancé have done this, share your paragraphs together.

Another expectation couples have is fidelity. They expect that they will be faithful to each other. After all, infidelity as commonly conceived would be out of the question in a Christian marriage. Fidelity, however, involves not only sexual faithfulness, but other areas of faithfulness as well. For example, some spouses are unfaithful to their mates through their work. The center of attention, which belongs to their spouses, is given to their jobs. Some spouses are unfaithful to their mates through their parents, fishing trips, golf, cars, church work, housekeeping, children, etc. You see, by putting any other person, possession, or activity (with the

exception of your relationship with Jesus Christ) before your spouse, you could be unfaithful to the marriage relationship.

What we need in marriage is creative fidelity. This means being sensitive to the needs of each other, supporting our partners, and being with them emotionally and physically.

Couples also expect their marriage to progress smoothly onward and upward without any major upheavals or adjustments. Consider the suggested outline of the three stages of marriage on the following page.

It has been suggested that most couples go through these three stages. What about you? Perhaps in your own relationship you have experienced some of the disenchantment stage already. Do you want to go through the full extent of the disenchantment stage as you see it expressed here? If not, then take some time to write out what you can do as an individual and what you can do as a couple to keep from going through all of the experiences of this stage. When you have finished writing, share your responses together.

Often many of our expectations come from our own homes and our own backgrounds. Complete the following statements and then share your responses with your fiancé.

1. This is what you need to know about my family life as I was growing up in order to understand me:

The Three Stages of Marriage

(and some words and ideas that go with these stages)[13]

Enchantment	Disenchantment	Maturity

Enchantment	Disenchantment	Maturity
On Cloud 9	Upset	Feet on the ground
Perfect	Terrible	I need you
Just right	Absolutely wrong	How do you see it?
Forever	I quit	Let's work it out
Infatuated	Hurt	I'll help you
Idolize	Put down	Encouragement
Impervious	Splintered	Whole
Fascinated	Irritated	Refreshed
Charmed	Wretched	Thankful
Captivated	Burdened	Free
Ecstatic	Uncomfortable	Comfortable
Thrilled	Bitter	Friendly
Preoccupied	Trapped	Growing
We've arrived	We'll never make it	Together, we can make it

2. If I could have changed one thing about my family life as I was growing up, it would have been . . .

3. Because I want or don't want this to occur in my own marriage and family life, I will . . .

4. My parents have influenced my attitudes toward marriage by . . .

5. Something from my parents' marriage that I would like to have in mine is . . .

6. Something from my parents' marriage that I prefer not having in mine is . . .

Talk with your fiancé and list, on a separate piece of paper, ten similarities and ten differences between their home and family life and yours. Discuss these together. How will any of these affect your own marriage?

Changes Will Come

Changes in marriage will happen. How will you adjust to them? Do you realize that even positive changes can disrupt a marriage relationship? A person who is married to a non-Christian and has prayed for many years for the spouse to accept the Lord suddenly discovers that the spouse has now accepted the Lord and has completely changed lifestyles. This upsets the Christian spouse. Why?

An alcoholic suddenly stops drinking and changes lifestyles, which is what the partner has been asking for, but now he or she is upset. Why?

A passive, submissive partner begins to be assertive in a positive way and becomes more involved with the family and the children. The other partner is a bit upset. Why?

Even though certain undesirable behaviors are occurring in a marriage relationship, the couple learns to adjust to them. When one makes a positive change, it upsets the equilibrium, and the spouse who has been asking for the change discovers that he or she must now change too. He or she must learn to adapt to the person, and that could be a bit uncomfortable. What was complained about is no longer there, so now the partner must face the change and learn how to relate to this "new" person.

The one spouse may ask, "If my partner could change all along, why did he [or she] wait so long and put me through all of this?" You might keep this in mind when you ask for a change. Remember this: The best way to help another to change is to make changes in your own life. The other person *may* change as he or she learns to relate to the new you.

Write how you would react to the following circumstances that could cause changes in your marriage.

1. a miscarriage

2. death of a child

3. major financial difficulty

4. being fired from a job

5. spouse wants to quit work and go back to school

6. major illness

7. a major lawsuit with potentially great financial loss and severe emotional stress

8. moving to an apartment instead of the home you were in for five years

9. living in the country instead of the city (or vice versa)

10. spouse is quitting job to start own business

11. husband and wife want to go to work and take the three children to daycare

12. child does not turn out the way you wanted

13. three more children than you planned on having

14. discovering that you cannot have children

15. a friend makes a pass at you or your spouse

16. in-laws turn hostile toward you

17. spouse has to work nights instead of days

18. car is stolen while on vacation

19. you are attracted to another person

20. spouse is no longer interested in spiritual things

Frustrations and disappointments are a part of life, but how they affect us is basically our choice. We can allow a disappointment to hamper us, destroy us, or even destroy our marriage. Another

response is to accept the disappointment, accept the hurt, discover what we can learn from it, and then make some new plans or find alternatives.

Read the following three passages of Scripture and write how you think these passages would help you accept and adjust to disappointments and changes.

> "Consider it all joy, my brethren, when you encounter various trials, knowing that the testing of your faith produces endurance" (James 1:2,3 NASB).

> "In this you greatly rejoice, even though now for a little while, if necessary, you have been distressed by various trials, that the proof of your faith, being more precious than gold which is perishable, even though tested by fire, may be found to result in praise and glory and honor at the revelation of Jesus Christ" (1 Peter 1:6,7 NASB).

> "Blessed is a man who perseveres under trial; for once he has been approved, he will receive the crown of life, which the Lord has promised to those who love Him" (James 1:12 NASB).

Look back at James 1:2,3. The word *count* or *consider* means "an internal attitude of heart and mind that causes the trial and circumstance of life to affect a person either adversely or beneficially." The verb tense used here means that this is a decisiveness of action, not just a passive giving up or resignation. Another interpretation of this word could be "make up your mind to regard adversities as something to welcome or be glad about." It is an attitude of the mind.

The word *trials* means "outward trouble or stress, or disappointments, sorrow, or hardships." These are situations that you had no part in bringing about. They are not sin. They just happened. They include all of the various sorts of trouble that we have in our lives.

The word *endurance*, or *patience* as it is sometimes translated, means "fortitude" or "the quality of being stabilized or remaining alive." It is, in a sense, a picture of standing firm under pressure rather than trying to escape.

How will the presence of Jesus Christ in your life help you to fulfill your expectations of marriage and accept the ones that are not fulfilled?

CHAPTER 5

A Vision Statement

❧

A good way to develop goals is to establish a "vision statement" for your marriage.

When you develop this vision statement:

- *Be specific*—A vision statement should have specific goals. Vague goals equal vague results. Quantify as much as possible.

- *Be positive*—A goal is something you want to have, not something you don't want. Focus on the positive.

There are many ways to think about vision. Vision could be described as *foresight*, with the significance of possessing a keen awareness of current circumstances and possibilities and of the value of learning from the past.

Vision can also be described as *seeing the invisible and making it visible*. It's having a picture held in your mind of the way things could or should be in the days ahead.[14]

Vision is also a *portrait of conditions that don't yet exist*. It's focusing on the future rather than getting bogged down by the past or present. Vision is the process of creating a better future with God's empowerment and direction.

Vision is specific, detailed, customized, sometimes time-specific, and measurable. Vision is a way of describing the activity and development of a marriage.[15] The vision you have for your marriage may be different from any other person's. Having a vision for your marriage is having a realistic dream for what you, your spouse, and your marriage can become under God's direction. And you need to seek what God wants for you and your marriage because, without His wisdom, what you achieve may be out of His will. You need His wisdom because, "the Lord knows the thoughts of man; he knows that they are futile" (Psalm 94:11 NIV).[16]

Here is an example of the marriage goals developed by one married couple:

We will show more respect for each other. We will show interest in one another when we first meet at the end of the day. We will give each other at least one compliment a day. We will listen to one another without interruption even when we don't agree with what the other is saying.

We will improve our sexual relationship. We will read a book on sex aloud to each other and work toward making our sexual experience creative, satisfying, and exciting most of the time. We will both communicate clearly before 8:00 P.M. if we are interested in sex that evening. We will also be more verbal before and during lovemaking.

We will demonstrate our love more, both verbally and nonverbally. We will both ask how we can help the other each day. We will say "I love you" to each other at least once a day. We will make love at least once a week. We will ask what the other wants to do on Friday and Saturday nights.

We will learn to be more flexible. We will learn to handle being spontaneous guests for dinner, and spontaneously having guests over for dinner.

We will see things from the other's perspective, giving ourselves two years to accomplish this. We will do a task the way our partner does it at least once before we encourage them to do it our way. We will work toward admitting when we're wrong and being less defensive.[17]

Goals in Marriage

Less than three percent of married couples have set goals for their marriage. Goals are vital. Unless you have something in mind that you want to work toward or achieve, you will not get very far. What goals do you have for your marriage? What do you want your marriage to become? What do you want it to reflect? What do you want from your marriage?

Now follow these directions concerning your goals.

List eight goals for your marriage on the goal wheel below. Write one goal in each of eight spaces. Then take one of the remaining spaces and write a goal that you would like to achieve within three to five years.

In the remaining space write a goal that you would like to see your fiancé achieve within three to five years. Remember, a goal should be reasonable, realistic, attainable, and have a time limit.

1. Place an asterisk (*) by six of the ten goals that you feel are the most important. Then rank them in order of importance.

2. Place a **0** by any two of the ten goals that you would be willing to forego if absolutely necessary.

3. Place a **$** by the ones that cost money.

4. Place a **P** by the ones you learned from your parents.

5. Place an **F** by the ones you think your fiancé also wrote down.

6. Explain in one sentence why your marriage goals are important to the health of your marriage.

7. Now share and discuss your goals with your fiancé.

8. Select two of your marriage goals and develop a plan to reach them. Also establish when you will come back to this exercise after you are married and redo it. It is important to periodically evaluate and determine goals because goals do change. Some may be short-range (to be achieved within three to six months) and some may be long-range (five to ten years).

9. How will the presence of Jesus Christ in your life assist you in setting and achieving your goals?

CHAPTER 6

Fulfilling Needs in Marriage

⸎

One of the motivating factors for marriage is the fulfillment of needs in one's life. It is admirable to say that we are marrying the other person in order to help him or her fulfill needs; but to be very honest, we hope and believe that our needs will be met too. In marriage counseling, one of the major complaints couples bring in is that of not having their needs met. Often one partner is attempting to meet the needs of the other but doesn't always know what the needs are or exactly how to meet them.

Thus we feel that it is important for a married person to define his or her needs specifically and then indicate how he or she would like the partner to respond in order to meet those needs. Some have asked, "Doesn't it take the romance out of marriage if you have to tell the other person exactly what you need?" Not really. In fact, it can increase the romance, since your spouse won't have to play the game of mind reading and try to figure out what you need and what you want!

Let's take a look at your needs. Write specifically what you think your needs are for each of the four areas on the next page. Then indicate what your spouse can do to help fulfill those needs.

Needs in Marriage

Physical:

Emotional:

Spiritual:

Social and intellectual:

What My Spouse Can Do to Help Fulfill These Needs

Now exchange your workbook with your fiancé, but cover up the section that shows what you would like your spouse-to-be to do to help meet your needs.

Read over each other's needs and then, on a separate piece of paper, write what you think you can do to meet these needs. When you have completed this assignment, reveal the covered portion and discover how perceptive you are in deciding how to meet the other's needs!

Years ago a psychologist named Abraham Maslow suggested that each person has certain basic needs in his or her life. He listed these needs in order of importance. First, a person seeks to fulfill his or her physiological needs. These are those things that are necessary in order to sustain life: food, water, oxygen, rest, etc. Second, a person seeks to fulfill safety needs, which involve the need for a safe environment, protection from harm, etc. Third, after having the first two sets of needs fulfilled, a person seeks to fulfill his or her need for love and belonging. This includes a desire for affectionate relationships with others. Fourth, a person seeks to fulfill his or her need for esteem. Esteem involves receiving recognition as a worthwhile person. Finally, after the other levels of needs are met, a person seeks to fulfill the need of self-actualization. This is the need to become the person one has the potential to become, to develop into a full, creative person.

Maslow's Levels of Needs

Most husbands and wives help to fulfill the first two levels of needs in each other—the physiological and safety needs. Most spouses, for example, make sure their mates have enough air, water, food, and rest. And most are concerned about keeping the car in good running order, making sure the house is clean and safe with proper lighting, ventilation, locks, and so on. But where most husbands

and wives fall down is in meeting their spouse's needs for love and belonging, esteem, and self-actualization.

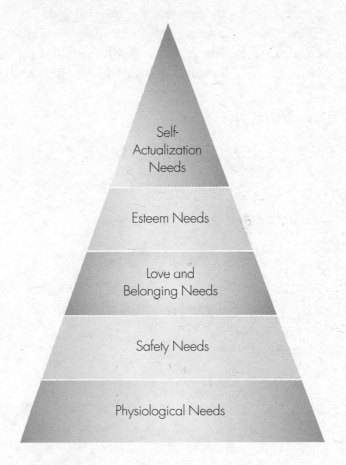

Looking at the above chart of the hierarchy of needs, complete the following sentences:

1. During our marriage, I will try to meet my fiancé's needs for love, esteem, and self-actualization by . . .

2. My fiancé can best meet my needs for love, esteem, and self-actualization by . . .

Now take your Bible and look for passages that verify that God has promised to meet every need on your list. Instead of relying on ourselves or our spouses to meet these needs, we find that God has given us promises for providing the stability we are seeking. You may want to start with the following references. To which area of needs do these relate?

1. Psalm 103:4

2. Matthew 6:33,34

3. Romans 5:8; 8:35,39

4. Ephesians 2:10

Within this classification of needs, the word *esteem* or *self-esteem* has arisen. This concept of self-esteem, or self-image, is one of the most important foundations of marriage. If one marries with a low self-esteem, a strain can be placed upon the marriage. You may be marrying in order to build your self-esteem or seeking to have your spouse give you a sense of meaning.

Our self-image or self-concept is often built upon our appearance. We ask, "How do I look?" Is your self-concept built upon your appearance? It is also probably built upon the following. To what degree does your self-concept depend on each of these? Write your responses.

1. Status: feeling important

2. Belonging: being wanted and accepted

3. Worthiness: feeling worthwhile and valuable

4. Competence: feeling adequate or more than adequate

Let's look specifically at the last three. Belonging rests on the voluntary attitude of others as they display their acceptance. It is a sense of security with others who love and accept you. Your fiancé probably accepts you, but what happens during times when you feel a lack of acceptance?

Worthiness rests on the introspective attitude of self-approval and being affirmed as a person of value. What happens when you don't feel that you approve of yourself?

Competence rests on the evaluations received in past relationships and on one's present sense of success.

What happens when you don't feel successful or when you've failed?

Think about this: Your worth is so great that if you had been the only person created upon the earth, God still would have sent His Son to die for you. You count that much to Him. Many of us strive for adequacy. God has declared us to be more than adequate in what He has done for us in His Son Jesus Christ.

In your relationship with God, you are assured of belongingness. In your relationship with the Son of God, you are assured of worthiness. In your relationship with the Holy Spirit, you have a secure sense of competence as He is your Comforter, Guide, and Source of Strength.

How will the presence of Jesus Christ in your life help you fulfill your needs and those of your spouse? How will His presence help you build your self-worth?

CHAPTER 7

Roles, Responsibilities, and Decision Making

※

What about the question of roles and responsibilities in marriage? Who does what and why? Does he or she do it? Is it because of tradition or because of what the church has said? Or is it because that's the way it was done in your parent's home? Or is it based on your skills and talents?

Failure to clarify the husband/wife roles in a romantic relationship is a major cause of future marital disruption. As a couple, you will be involved in an almost endless number of activities and responsibilities. Each couple should discuss together and decide who is most competent to do each task. Tasks should not be assigned on the basis of parental example, the expectations of your social group, or tradition. When an individual's abilities, training, and temperament make it difficult or unnecessary to follow an established cultural norm for a role, you will need to have the strength to establish your own style of working together.

It is imperative that you deliberately and mutually develop the rules and guidelines for your relationship as husband and wife. This clear assignment of authority and responsibility does not create a rigid relationship but allows flexibility and order in what could become a chaotic mess.

Let's spend some time now thinking about your role as a wife or husband.

A Woman's Place?

Property—Wife has almost no rights and privileges compared to those of the husband. Husband is the family provider. Often the wife is viewed as property and an outlet for the husband's sexual expression.

Complement—Wife's rights have increased. Marriage is the wife's central life interest. Husband is chief provider and has more authority than wife. She is a friend to her husband. He achieves; she supports him.

Junior Partner—Wife's rights increase because she works outside the home for pay. Her main motive is to improve the family's lifestyle. She has more authority (rights) than a stay-at-home wife.

Equal Partner—Wife and husband share equal rights and responsibilities.

When both of you have completed the following chart, share your responses.

On the chart below, place your initials below the mark
that indicates your vision of your spouse's role in marriage.
Then place your spouse's initials where you think he or she would.

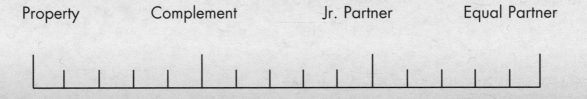

| Property | Complement | Jr. Partner | Equal Partner |

Complete the following sentences and discuss them.

1. In marriage, I believe a "role" is . . .

2. My main role in marriage will be . . .

3. I formed this belief about my role when . . .

4. My mate's role will be . . .

5. In marriage, a wife should . . .

6. In marriage, a husband should . . .

7. I can best help my mate fulfill his or her role by . . .

Use a separate piece of paper for the Role Concepts Comparison that follows. Read each statement and write the appropriate number indicating what you believe about each one. Then go back and indicate how you think your fiancé responded to each statement. Finally, for each one, write where you obtained your belief—from your parents, pastor, friends, or your own idea.

Role Concepts Comparison

What do you believe about roles in marriage? Circle the number that best reflects your position using these guidelines:

(1) strongly agree

(2) mildly agree

(3) not sure

(4) mildly disagree

(5) strongly disagree

Wife		*Husband*
1 2 3 4 5	**A.** The husband is the head of the home.	1 2 3 4 5
1 2 3 4 5	**B.** The wife should not be employed outside the home.	1 2 3 4 5
1 2 3 4 5	**C.** The husband should help regularly with the household chores.	1 2 3 4 5
1 2 3 4 5	**D.** It is all right for the wife to initiate love-making.	1 2 3 4 5
1 2 3 4 5	**E.** The husband and wife should plan the budget and manage money matters together.	1 2 3 4 5
1 2 3 4 5	**F.** Neither the husband nor the wife should purchase an item costing more than $100 without consulting the other.	1 2 3 4 5
1 2 3 4 5	**G.** The husband is the one responsible for disciplining the children.	1 2 3 4 5
1 2 3 4 5	**H.** The wife can choose an "outside the home" career if she wants.	1 2 3 4 5

Wife		*Husband*
1 2 3 4 5	**I.** The wife is responsible for keeping the house neat and clean.	1 2 3 4 5
1 2 3 4 5	**J.** The husband should plan a date night with his wife twice a month.	1 2 3 4 5
1 2 3 4 5	**K.** The wife is just as responsible for the children's discipline as the husband.	1 2 3 4 5
1 2 3 4 5	**L.** It is the husband's job to do the yard work.	1 2 3 4 5
1 2 3 4 5	**M.** The wife should be the one who teaches values to the children.	1 2 3 4 5
1 2 3 4 5	**N.** Children should be allowed to help plan family activities.	1 2 3 4 5
1 2 3 4 5	**O.** Children develop better in a home with parents who are strict disciplinarians.	1 2 3 4 5
1 2 3 4 5	**P.** All income should be pooled together with equal access.	1 2 3 4 5
1 2 3 4 5	**Q.** The husband and wife should each have at least one night a week out with friends.	1 2 3 4 5
1 2 3 4 5	**R.** The wife should always be the one to cook.	1 2 3 4 5
1 2 3 4 5	**S.** The husband's primary responsibility is to his job; the wife's primary responsibility is to the home and children.	1 2 3 4 5

What does the Word of God say concerning the role of the wife and the role of the husband? Read Ephesians 5:21-33.

1. What one word summarizes a wife's responsibility to her husband? Compare 1 Peter 3:1.

2. What do the words "as unto the Lord" (verse 22 KJV) suggest about the wife's role?

3. Are there any limits placed upon the wife's submission by Colossians 3:18 and Acts 5:29?

4. According to verse 33, what should the wife's attitude be toward her husband and what does this mean in everyday life?

5. What does the word *submission* mean to you?

Submission does not mean that the wife is inferior nor does it stifle her initiative. It does not limit her in any way. Read Proverbs 31:10-31. Make a list on a separate piece of paper of the ways the woman in Proverbs 31 uses her abilities.

What is the husband's role? Is submission part of his role and function? What does Ephesians 5:21 say?

1. Study Ephesians 5:22-33. What two words in this section summarize the husband's responsibility? Compare verse 23 with verse 25. See Philippians 2:4.

2. What example should the husband exhibit as he leads in the marriage relationship? Compare Ephesians 5:23 with 1:22. In light of this, for whose benefit should the headship of the husband be exercised?

3. For whose benefit is the headship of Christ exercised? Compare Ephesians 1:22 and 5:25-27. In light of this, for whose benefit should the headship of the husband be exercised?

4. What are the ways in which Christ loved the church? Relate each of these to the way a husband should love his wife.

5. In Proverbs 31 we see that the wife has been given great responsibility and is able to use her gifts. What gifts and abilities does your wife-to-be have that you do not?

6. In Proverbs 31:28,29, the husband praises and expresses appreciation to his wife. Is this one reason she is so capable?

Perhaps you are already getting the idea that in marriage each one gives to and receives from the other. Marriage is built upon each person being a complement to the other. Dr. Dwight Small expressed it in this way:

When a man and a woman unite in marriage, humanity experiences a restoration to wholeness. The glory of the man is the acknowledgment that woman was created for him; the glory of the woman is the acknowledgment that man is incomplete without her. The humility of the woman is the acknowledgment that she was made for man; the humility of the man is the acknowledgment that he is incomplete without her. Both share equal dignity, honor, and worth.

Each shares humility before the other. Each is necessarily the completion of the other; each is necessarily dependent upon the other.[18]

Earlier you discovered that the role of the husband is that of a servant. What are some creative ways that a husband can be a loving leader-servant?

1.

2.

3.

4.

5.

6.

7.

8.

9.

10.

Decision Making

Who makes the decisions in the marital relationship? Perhaps the question is not who does or who should, but who is best qualified. Who in the marital relationship exerts the most influence upon the other or carries more weight in deciding?

Decision-Making Percentages

On a separate piece of paper, describe the decision-making process you think you will have in your marriage by putting the percentage of influence that you will have and that your spouse will have for various issues. The total for each decision must be 100 percent.

After both of you have done this, exchange papers, compare your answers, and discuss the results together.

Some questions to consider are: Will each make decisions in the areas where he or she is most gifted? Will each person have sufficient opportunity to give what he or she has to offer? What are the reasons for allotting the percentages of influence as you did?

Every couple directly or indirectly establishes a pattern for reaching marital decisions. Many of these patterns are ineffective or self-defeating. Some bring about lingering feelings of resentment. The majority of couples have not considered how they arrive at decisions.

	Her Vote	His Vote
Choice of new car	_____	_____
Choice of home	_____	_____
Choice of furniture	_____	_____
Choice of your own wardrobe	_____	_____
Choice of vacation spots	_____	_____
Choice of decor for the home	_____	_____
Choice of mutual friends	_____	_____
Choice of entertainment	_____	_____
Choice of church	_____	_____

	Her Vote	His Vote
Choice of child-rearing practices	_____	_____
Choice of TV shows.	_____	_____
Choice of home menu	_____	_____
Choice of number of children.	_____	_____
Choice of where we live.	_____	_____
Choice of husband's vocation	_____	_____
Choice of wife's vocation	_____	_____
Choice of determining for what and how the money is spent	_____	_____

Write your answers to the following questions and then discuss how well you have considered the decision-making process.

1. Who made most of the decisions in your family? How would your fiancé answer this question?

2. Have you established guidelines to distinguish between major and minor decisions? If so, what are they?

3. What procedure will you follow when there is an impasse and a decision must be made?

4. How will you decide upon responsibilities for household chores?

5. In what areas of family life will you make decisions without consulting your spouse? Who decided this policy? How did you arrive at this decision?

6. Will you make the decisions that you want to make or the ones that your spouse does not want to make?

7. Will you have any "veto power" over your spouse's decisions? If so, what is the basis for it? How did you arrive at this decision?

How did you do in answering these questions? Most couples have never thought them through, and yet they are vital to an understanding of the marital relationship.

Answer these questions and then compare your responses with those of your fiancé.

1. I'm afraid to make decisions when . . .

2. I'm afraid to have my fiancé make decisions when . . .

3. I'd like to make decisions when . . .

4. I'd like my fiancé to make decisions when . . .

5. I want to make decisions in the area of . . .

6. I want my fiancé to make decisions in the area of . . .

Consider these thoughts about the roles of the husband and wife in decision making:

"The principle of mutuality of submissiveness in marriage is similar to the pattern of submissiveness between the members of the Body of Christ. There are times in the Body when it is appropriate for one member to exercise leadership over the other members as a function of his or her spiritual gift (1 Corinthians 12:14-26).

"No single spiritual gift automatically qualifies a member to be the leader or ultimate decision maker all of the time. That position belongs to the head, Jesus Himself. Likewise in marriage, in which there is mutuality of submissiveness, the role of leadership is assigned not according to some decree from God, or on the basis of 'maleness' or 'femaleness,' but on the basis of the leadership role the partner has been assigned by the mutual decision of the marriage. The skill of a Christian marriage lies in the negotiation and assignment of these leadership roles on the basis of the abilities of the partners."[19]

"In the marriage the husband has the office of head. That simply means he has the responsibility and authority to call the marriage—his wife as well as himself—to obey the norm of troth. If he faithfully exercises his office, both he and his wife will be freed to be themselves. As the head, the husband is called to take the lead in mutually examining the marriage to see if it is developing according to its long-range goals.

"Clearly, headship has nothing to do with being boss. The husband can only command the wife to live up to what the two of them mutually pledged when they were married.

Likewise, if the husband neglects his office, the wife ought to call the husband back to their mutual vows.

"Neither does headship imply inferiority or superiority. Rather, headship is a special office of service so that the marriage may thrive and grow. Headship does not mean that the husband leads or decides in every detail. Once a man and woman have decided which vision of life is going to [be the] norm [in] their activities in their marriage, they can leave the decisions in day-to-day affairs to the partner with the appropriate talents, temperaments, and situations. The husband's role is to be on guard continually so that the 'little' things do not develop into the kinds of patterns that undermine the entire marriage."[20]

How will the presence of Jesus Christ in your life help you in the process of decision making and discovering your gifts in marriage?

CHAPTER 8

In-Laws or Outlaws—
It's Your Choice

୬୬

You are about to become an in-law. (This term refers to children- as well as parents-in-law.) What does the word *in-law* mean to you? Write your definition and share it with your fiancé.

What examples of in-laws do we find in the Scriptures? Read the following three selections and ask yourself, "How would I have responded if I had been in the same situation?"

1. Genesis 26:34–27:46

2. Exodus 18:13-24

3. Ruth

Describe the ideal in-law relationship from your perspective. Share this with your fiancé.

Describe what you think would be the ideal in-law relationship from your parents' perspective and from that of your fiancé's parents.

Here are 20 of the most important questions concerning in-laws. Answer them, and then share your answers with your fiancé.

1. Genesis 2:24; Matthew 19:5; Mark 10:7,8; and Ephesians 5:31 all say the same thing. What does the word *leave* mean to you?

2. If your parents were to help you get started financially, what might they expect in return?

3. How do your parents feel about your plans for marriage?

4. What emotional ties with your parents interfere with your relationship? Explain.

5. How do you think your future in-laws view you?

6. What would you consider to be "interference" by your future in-laws?

7. How did you get along with your mother and father during your childhood?

8. Describe your present relationship with your mother and father.

9. How do you think your parents view your partner?

10. What one thing about your partner's parents do you dislike?

11. What three things about your partner's parents do you really appreciate?

12. What customs in your home differ from those in your partner's home?

13. Describe how and where you would like to spend your first Thanksgiving and Christmas.

14. What have you done in the past to let both your own parents and your future in-laws know they are important to you?

15. During the past two weeks, what have you done to express your positive feelings toward your parents and your future in-laws?

16. What new things could you say or do that would let your parents and your future in-laws know they are important to you?

17. Describe what you have done to discover from your parents or future in-laws what kind of relationship they expect from you and your fiancé (such as how often to visit or call, their involvement in disciplining your children, etc.).

    What can you do about this in the future if it changes?

18. In the past, how have you helped your parents or future in-laws meet their own needs and develop greater meaning in life?

    How can you help them in the future?

19. In the past, what have you done with your parents or future in-laws to make it easier for them to demonstrate love toward you as a couple?

    How can you improve on this in the future?

20. What have you done in the past to assist your parents or future in-laws to receive love from you? What have you done to demonstrate love to them?

    Consider this: What would happen if you were to write your future in-laws a letter sharing with them why you are looking forward to having them as your in-laws and thanking them for providing your fiancé for you? It may increase the satisfaction in your future relationship.

    In what way will the presence of Jesus Christ in your life help you in building positive in-law relationships?

CHAPTER 9

Communication

⁓

Communication is to love what blood is to life. Have you ever thought about it in that way before? It is impossible to have any kind of relationship unless there is communication. That is true for you and your fiancé and for your relationship with God.

How would you define *communication?* What do you think the word means? Write your definition and then share your answer with your fiancé.

Now define *listening* and again share your definition.

Turn to the end of this section (page 61) and read a definition of communication and a definition of listening.

How important is communication? Think about this.

"If there is any indispensable insight with which a young married couple should begin their life together, it is that they should try to keep open, at all cost, the lines of communication between them."[21]

"A marriage can be likened to a large house with many rooms to which a couple fall heir on their wedding day. Their hope is to use and enjoy these rooms, as we do the rooms in a comfortable home, so that they will serve the many activities that make up their shared life. But in many marriages, doors are found to be locked—they represent areas in the relationship which the couple are unable to explore together. Attempts to open these doors lead to failure and frustration. The right key cannot be found. So the couple resign themselves to living together in only a few rooms that can be opened easily, leaving the rest of the house, with all its promising possibilities, unexplored and unused.

"There is, however, a master key that will open every door. It is not easy to find. Or, more correctly, it has to be forged by the couple together, and this can be very difficult. It is the great art of effective marital communication."[22]

Let's consider another aspect of communication. In our communication we send messages. Every message has three components: the actual content, the tone of voice, and the nonverbal communication. With changes in the tone of voice or in the nonverbal component, it is possible to express many different messages using the same word, statement, or question. Nonverbal communication includes facial expressions, body postures, and actions. An example of nonverbal communication which should be avoided is holding a book in front of one's face while talking.

The three components of communication must be complementary. One researcher has suggested the following breakdown of the importance of the three components.[23] The percentages indicate how much of the message is sent through each one.

Content / 7%

Tone / 38%

Nonverbal / 55%

Confusing messages are often sent because the three components contradict one another.

Take a minute and think about how you communicate nonverbally. Then write how your fiancé communicates nonverbally.

After you have done this, write what you think your nonverbal communication means to the other person and what you think your fiancé's nonverbal communication means. Compare and discuss your responses.

Our nonverbal communication and tone of voice are essential elements in conveying our messages. If you are not aware of your tone of voice, you may want to record some of your conversations. Then play them back and pay attention to your tone of voice and what it implies.

How will you communicate in the following situations?

1. It's Saturday. Your spouse asks you to shop for something, but you really don't want to go. You say:

2. You are trying to watch your favorite TV program but your spouse is continually interrupting and asking you questions. The program is at the crucial part, and you don't want to miss it. You say:

3. You are describing to your spouse the most exciting event of the day. Right in the middle of it, your spouse yawns and says, "I think I'll go get a cup of coffee." You say:

4. Your spouse serves you breakfast. You notice that the bacon is overcooked, which you don't like. The toast is served lightly toasted with fresh butter, which is exactly what you like. You say:

5. After dinner your spouse asks you if you would do the dishes tonight since he or she is so tired. You, too, are tired and were looking forward to relaxing. Usually you both do them together. You say:

6. You have just had an argument with one of the children and you realize that you are wrong. It is not easy to apologize to family members because they usually rub it in. You say:

What does the Word of God say about communication? Look up the passages listed and write the key thought for each one. You will notice that the verses are listed in groupings as there is a central theme in each group. See if you can discover the central thought for each group and write it as a summary.

1. Proverbs 11:9
   Proverbs 12:18
   Proverbs 15:4
   Proverbs 18:8
   Proverbs 18:21
   Proverbs 25:11
   Proverbs 26:22
   James 3:8-10
   1 Peter 3:10

2. Proverbs 4:20-23
   Proverbs 6:12,14,18

Proverbs 15:28
Proverbs 16:2
Proverbs 16:23

3. Proverbs 15:31
   Proverbs 18:13
   Proverbs 18:15
   Proverbs 19:20
   Proverbs 21:28
   James 1:19

4. Proverbs 12:18
   Proverbs 14:29
   Proverbs 15:28
   Proverbs 16:32
   Proverbs 21:23
   Proverbs 26:4
   Proverbs 29:20

5. Proverbs 15:23
   Proverbs 25:11

6. Proverbs 10:19
   Proverbs 11:12,13
   Proverbs 13:3
   Proverbs 17:27,28
   Proverbs 18:2
   Proverbs 20:19
   Proverbs 21:23

7. Proverbs 17:9
   Proverbs 21:9

8. Proverbs 15:1
   Proverbs 15:4
   Proverbs 16:1
   Proverbs 25:15

9. Proverbs 12:16
   Proverbs 19:11

10. Proverbs 12:17,22
    Proverbs 16:13
    Proverbs 19:5
    Proverbs 26:18,19
    Proverbs 26:22
    Proverbs 28:23
    Proverbs 29:5
    Ephesians 4:15,25
    Colossians 3:9

Let's see what kind of communicator you are and discover how much you know about your fiancé. Imagine that you are interviewing a stranger. Your task is to ask the other person any question you want about marriage, dating experiences, childhood, hobbies, likes and dislikes, religious views, feelings about self, looks, etc. Keep in mind that you know nothing about the other person. Construct your questions so that you assume nothing.

Keep your opinions out. When you have completed the interview, change roles and have your fiancé interview you.

In his book *Why Am I Afraid to Tell You Who I Am?* John Powell states that we communicate on five different levels, from shallow clichés to deep personal sharing. Hang-ups, such as fear, apathy, and a poor self-image, keep us at the shallow level. If we can be freed from our restrictions, we can move to the deeper, more meaningful level.

Here are five levels of communication.

Level Five: Cliché Conversation. This type of talk is very safe. We use phrases such as "How are you?" "How's the dog?" "Where have you been?" "I like your dress." In this type of conversation there is no personal sharing. Each person remains safely behind his defenses.

Level Four: Reporting the Facts About Others. In this kind of conversation we are content to tell others what someone else has said, but we offer no personal information on these facts. We report the facts like the six o'clock news. We share gossip and little narrations, but we do not commit ourselves as to how we feel about them.

Level Three: Ideas and Judgments. Real communication begins to unfold here. The person is willing to step out of his solitary confinement and risk telling some of his ideas and decisions. He is still cautious. If he senses that what he is saying is not being accepted, he will retreat.

Level Two: Feelings or Emotions. At this level the person shares how he feels about facts, ideas, and judgments. His feelings underneath these areas are revealed. For a person to really share himself with another individual he must move to the level of sharing his feelings.

Level One: Complete Emotional and Personal Communication. All deep relationships must be based on absolute openness and honesty. This may be difficult to achieve because it involves risk—the risk of being rejected. But it is vital if relationships are to grow. There will be times when this type of communication is not as complete as it could be.[24]

Take the time right now to write down your answers to these questions:

1. What are some of the reasons why a person might respond only at level five or level four?

2. When do you feel most like responding at levels two and one?

3. At what level do you usually respond?

4. At what level does your fiancé usually respond?

5. On which level do you usually share with God?

6. Describe a time when you really felt that you communicated with God.

Persons who communicate primarily on a cognitive or thinking level deal mainly with factual data. They like to talk about such topics as sports, the stock market, money, houses, jobs, etc., keeping the subject of conversation out of the emotional area. Usually they are quite uncomfortable dealing with issues that elicit feelings, especially unpleasant feelings such as anger. Consequently they avoid talking about subjects that involve love, fear, and anger. These persons have difficulty, then, being warm and supportive of their spouses.

Others communicate more on the feeling level. They tire easily of purely factual data and feel a need to share feelings, especially with their spouses. They feel that the atmosphere between husband and wife must be as free as possible from unpleasant feelings like tension, anger, and resentment. So, of course, they want to talk about these emotional things, resolve conflicts with their spouses, clear the air, and keep things pleasant between them.

Of course no one is completely cognitive or completely emotional. Where are you and where is your fiancé? On the diagram below indicate (1) where you think you are, (2) where you think your fiancé is, and (3) where you think your fiancé would place you.

A person on the left side of the graph, who shares more feelings, is not less bright or less intellectual. This person is simply aware of his/her feelings and is usually better able to do something about them.

Surprisingly, the so-called cognitive person (on the right) is controlled by his feelings just as is the so-called emotional person, but he or she doesn't realize it. For example, the stiff, formal intellectual

Emotional   Cognitive

has deep feelings also but uses enormous energy to keep them buried so he or she won't be bothered with them. Unfortunately they do bother him or her. Whenever someone "emotional" is around asking for affection and warmth, the intellectual might be unable to respond and be angered that his or her equilibrium has been disturbed.[25]

Communication Definitions

Communication is the process of sharing yourself, both verbally and nonverbally, in such a way that the other person can both accept and understand what you are sharing.

What is listening? Paul Tournier said, "How beautiful, how grand and liberating this experience is, when people learn to help each other. It is impossible to overemphasize the immense need humans have to be really listened to. Listen to all the conversations of our world, between nations as well as those between couples. They are, for the most part, dialogues of the deaf."[26]

Read these thoughts about listening:

"Any story sounds true until someone tells the other side and sets the record straight" (Proverbs 18:17 TLB).

"The wise man learns by listening; the simpleton can learn only by seeing scorners punished" (Proverbs 21:11 TLB).

"He who answers a matter before he hears the facts, it is folly and shame to him" (Proverbs 18:13, AMP).

"Let every man be quick to hear (a ready listener) . . ." (James 1:19 AMP).

What do we mean by listening? When we are truly listening to another person, we are not thinking about what we are going to say when he or she stops talking. We are not busy formulating our response. We are concentrating on what is being said. Listening is also complete acceptance without judgment of what is said or how it is said. Often we fail to hear the message because we don't like the message or the tone of voice. We react and miss the meaning of what was being shared.

By acceptance, we do not mean agreeing with everything that is being said. Acceptance means understanding that what the other person is saying is something he or she feels. Real listening means that we should be able to repeat both what the other person has said *and* what we thought he or she was feeling when speaking to us.

It is important to become proficient in communication. You may want to read *Bringing Out the Best in Your Husband* or *Bringing Out the Best in Your Wife* by H. Norman Wright. These books can be ordered online or by telephone at Christian Marriage Enrichment, 800-875-7560, www.hnormanwright.com.

CHAPTER 10

Conflict
(or "Sound the Battle Cry!")

❧

Are you anticipating conflict in your marriage? If not, you may be in for a surprise. Conflict is a fact of life. It has been defined as a clash, contention, or sharp disagreement over interests, ideas, etc. Why does conflict occur? The answer is simply that we are human beings—imperfect people whom God graciously loves in spite of our imperfections. Each of us has our own desires, wants, needs, and goals. Whenever any of these differ from those of another, conflict may occur. Our beliefs, ideas, attitudes, feelings, and behaviors will be different. The differences themselves are not the problem, but rather our reaction to them.

Many times disagreements or conflicts do not need to be completely resolved. An example may be a disagreement over political philosophy. This type of disagreement could continue indefinitely and need not destroy the overall marital relationship.

1. List some of the issues you and your fiancé disagree on that do not need to be completely resolved.

2. What does "completely resolved" mean to you?

3. Make a list of some issues on which you disagree that do need solutions—those on which more time needs to be spent exploring alternatives.

4. Select one of the issues on which more time needs to be spent. Write an explanation of the situation as you see it.

5. Some people have learned to use behavioral, nonviolent weapons in dealing with conflict. What are some unfair weapons?

6. What effect does anger have upon resolving a conflict? What effect does anger have upon a marriage?

Remember that anger comes about for three basic reasons: hurt, fear, and frustration. (If you would like to explore this topic further, read *Winning over Your Emotions* by H. Norman Wright and *30 Days to Taming Your Anger* by Deborah Smith Pegues.)

What do the following verses have to say about the right way to handle anger?

1. Psalm 37:1-11

2. Proverbs 14:29

3. Proverbs 15:1

4. Proverbs 15:28

5. Proverbs 16:32

6. Proverbs 19:11

7. Proverbs 25:28

8. Proverbs 29:11

9. Matthew 5:43,44

10. Romans 8:28,29

11. Romans 12:19,21

12. Galatians 5:16-23

13. Ephesians 4:26

14. Ephesians 4:29

15. Ephesians 4:32

What causes conflicts? (See James 4:1-3.)

Take a look at your relationship.

1. Describe a recent or current conflict between you and your fiancé.

2. What do you believe caused the conflict? What was the outcome? What did it accomplish?

3. How did you create or contribute to the conflict?

4. Imagine that you are seeing the conflict from the other person's perspective. How would your fiancé describe the conflict?

5. If you could go through the same conflict again, how would you handle it?

Remember: Conflict is a natural part of growth and family living. Many conflicts are simply symptoms of something else. Most people do not deal openly with conflict because no one has ever taught them effective ways. On the positive side, conflict does provide opportunity for growth in a relationship. Unresolved and buried conflicts arise from their graves and interfere with growth and satisfying relationships.

Dealing with Conflicts

What choices do we have in dealing with conflicts? James Fairfield has suggested five styles of dealing with conflict.[27]

The first is to *withdraw*. If you have a tendency to view conflict as a hopeless inevitability that you can do little to control, you may not even try. You may withdraw physically by leaving the scene or you may leave psychologically.

If you feel that you must always look after your own interests or your self-concept is threatened in a conflict, you may choose to *win*. No matter what the cost, you must win. Domination is usually reflected in this style; personal relationships take second place.

"Giving in to get along" is another style. You may not like it, but rather than risk a confrontation you choose to *yield*.

"Give a little to get a little" is called *compromise*. You may find that it is important to let up on some of your demands or ideas in order to help the other person give a little. You don't want to win all the time nor do you want the other person to win all the time.

A person may choose to *resolve* conflicts. In this style of dealing with conflicts, a situation, attitude, or behavior is changed by open and direct communication.

1. Select your usual style of dealing with conflicts.

2. Select your fiancé's usual style.

Withdrew:

Won:

3. Describe a situation in which you withdrew from a conflict.

Yielded:

Compromised:

4. Describe a situation in which you won a conflict.

Resolved:

5. Describe a situation in which you yielded in a conflict.

9. How did you feel about yourself in each situation?

Withdrew:

Won:

6. Describe a situation in which you compromised in a conflict.

Yielded:

Compromised:

Resolved:

7. Describe a situation in which you resolved a conflict.

10. Did the result eventually bring about a more peaceful atmosphere in each case?

8. Describe how each solution affected the feelings of others toward you.

What style did Jesus use? What styles of handling conflict do we find in the Scriptures? Take a few minutes and read the following accounts of conflict. Try to determine the methods used at that time. Write down the various styles you observe.

1. Genesis 4

2. 1 Samuel 20:30-34

3. Matthew 15:10-20

4. Mark 11:11-19

5. Luke 23:18-49

6. John 8:1-11

7. John 11:11-19

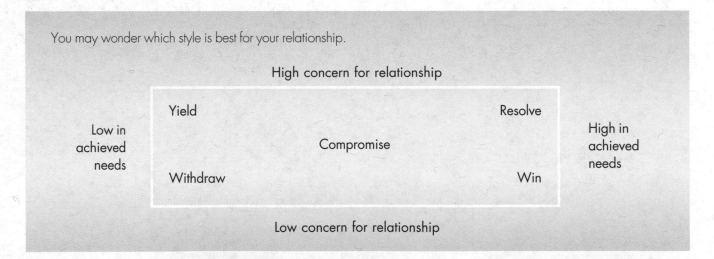

You may wonder which style is best for your relationship.

High concern for relationship

Yield   Resolve

Low in   High in
achieved   Compromise   achieved
needs   needs

Withdraw   Win

Low concern for relationship

As you can see from the diagram above, *withdraw* has the lowest value because the person gives up on meeting the goals and developing the relationship. The relationship is turned off. If this style is used temporarily as a cooling off step toward *resolve*, it is beneficial. There may be times when the discussion is so heated and out of control that withdrawing is best. But it is important to make a definite and specific commitment to discuss and resolve the conflict.

The *win* method achieves the goal but can sacrifice the relationship. In a family, personal relationships are just as important or more important than the goal.

Yielding works just the other way in that the relationship is maintained but the goals are sacrificed.

Compromise attempts to work out some needs but the bargaining involved may mean that you compromise some of your own values. If you have some basic convictions about the type of young men that your daughter dates and you begin to compromise your standards in order to have greater harmony, what does that do?

Naturally, the highest value or style is *resolve* because, in the final analysis, relationships are strengthened as you seek to meet personal needs.

How then can we resolve conflicts? Consider trying and applying these principles:

1. Instead of demanding that you be heard, listen carefully to the other person (see Proverbs 18:13 and James 1:19). Any changes that one person wants to see in another must be heard and understood.

2. Select an appropriate time. "A man has joy in making an apt answer, and a word spoken at the right moment, how good it is" (Proverbs 15:23 AMP).

3. Define the problem. How do you define the problem and how does the other person define it?

4. Define the areas of agreement and disagreement.

5. Here comes the difficult part. A few conflicts *may* be just one-sided, but most involve contributions from both sides. Identify your contribution to the problem. When you accept some responsibility for a problem, the other sees a willingness to cooperate and will probably be much more open to the discussion.

6. The next step is to state positively what behaviors on your part would probably help, and to be willing to ask for the other person's opinion. As they share with you, be open to their feelings, observations, and suggestions. Watch out for defensiveness.

Read the following passages in The Living Bible. What do these verses say?

1. Proverbs 13:18

2. Proverbs 23:12

3. Proverbs 25:12

4. Proverbs 28:13

How will the presence of Jesus Christ in your life help you deal with conflict?

CHAPTER 11

Finances

〜〜〜

Money! It takes money to eat and to pay the rent, the tax collector, the grocer, etc. Your attitude toward money and past lifestyle may need adjustments when you marry. Financial disruption and difficulties in marriage can place a strain upon the marital relationship. The next several exercises have been designed to help you determine what is important to you in terms of finances and enable you to make realistic plans.

First, let's see how aware you are of how much items cost today.

"You paid *how much* for that?"

Secret thoughts of a husband: "I just can't understand why my wife is always short of money. Now if I took over, things would be more efficient and there would be money to spare."

A wife broods: "I don't know why my husband says he can't take me out more often. His expenses aren't that high."

Do you confess to thinking like that occasionally? Here is your chance to show how much you know about the day-to-day money problems your fiancé will face. This quiz is divided into two sections, one for each partner. Each of you is asked to approximate the cost of twenty items or services that the other will probably pay for. Here are the rules.

Women ask their husbands-to-be the questions headed "For Men." Men ask their wives-to-be the questions headed "For Women." In some cases a price range rather than the approximate cost may be allowed.

Score four points for each correct answer. Don't be too strict. Give your fiancé credit for a correct answer if he or she comes within, say, 10 percent of what you think is the right amount.

If you want to compare scores, go ahead—but that's not the point of the quiz. The idea is simply to show how well you understand your partner's expenses. And maybe the quiz will act as a caution: Don't beef about somebody's spending habits until you know what you are talking about.

How much would you have to pay for these?

For Men	For Women
1. A woman's business suit	1. A man's business suit
2. A haircut (with perm if applicable)	2. A haircut (with perm if applicable)
3. A week's groceries for two people	3. A week's groceries for two people
4. Two tickets to a football game or the symphony	4. Two tickets to a football game or the symphony
5. One month's costs of physical fitness (health club, clothes, etc.)	5. One month's cost of physical fitness (health club, clothes, etc.)
6. A pair of living room curtains	6. New seat covers for a car
7. A "drive-through" oil change	7. A complete car tune-up
8. Makeup supplies	8. Shaving supplies
9. A woman's raincoat	9. A man's raincoat
10. A pair of nylons	10. A pair of men's dress socks
11. A pair of kid's Levi's	11. A pair of kid's Levi's
12. A set of 8 water glasses	12. A set of 8 water glasses
13. A woman's purse	13. A man's wallet
14. Vertical blinds for a sliding glass door	14. Vertical blinds for a sliding glass door
15. New snow skis	15. A graphite fishing rod
16. A tall living-room lamp	16. A six-foot aluminum stepladder
17. A good frying pan	17. A good frying pan
18. A sewing machine	18. A 20-inch power lawnmower
19. Bathroom scales	19. Bathroom scales
20. An affordable mid-size car	20. An affordable mid-size car

Financial Goals

Money and Control

Money can be used as power. People can use it to manipulate others and show a lack of trust. For example, one partner can demonstrate distrust by closely questioning all the receipts of the other. This is not how to start a marriage.

Money May Be Your Source of Status

Money can also be used as a source of status or self-esteem. It's called "trying to keep up with the neighbors." It's the way that some people gain their identity. This does not give you what you want—satisfaction and contentment.

One Problem

The shopaholic. This is someone who overspends in a compulsive way. This isn't careful, shop-the-sales-type buying, but an almost uncontrollable, impulse-buying habit. Take the following test to evaluate where you stand.

Shopping Quiz

(N = No; OC = Occasionally; O = Often; VO = Very Often)

_____ Shopping is my most frequent form of entertainment. I feel anxious when I'm not shopping.

_____ Shopping takes the place of talking, feeling, and dealing with the unpleasant realities of life.

_____ I argue with others about my shopping and spending habits.

_____ I repeatedly buy things I neither need nor want.

_____ I get a rush or a high from even thinking about shopping.

_____ I am concerned about how often I shop, but I continue to shop anyway.

_____ I minimize my purchases or hide them from people.

_____ I buy clothing that doesn't fit my lifestyle, and rarely, if ever, use those items.

What Are Your Financial Goals and Priorities?

List in order of importance five areas where you should currently be spending your money.

1) _____

2) _____

3) _____

4) _____

5) _____

If someone gave you a gift of $10,000, how would you spend it?

1) _____

2) _____

3) _____

4) _____

5) _____

How would your fiancé spend it?

1) _____

2) _____

3) _____

4) _____

5) _____

Family Financial Background

1. Which of these describes how you felt about money as you were growing up?

   _____ I always felt secure that there would be enough money for whatever I needed and wanted.

   _____ I never felt certain my parents would have enough money to give me what I wanted or needed.

   _____ I always felt that I had less than my friends had.

   _____ I felt the people around me placed too much importance on money.

   _____ I was embarrassed by being seen as a "rich kid."

   _____ I knew I wanted to grow up to have a lot of money.

   _____ Other: _____.

2. Which of these describes how you think your fiancé felt about money as he or she was growing up?

   _____ My fiancé always felt secure that there would be enough money to cover needs and wants.

   _____ My fiancé never felt certain that there would be enough money to cover needs and wants.

   _____ My fiancé always felt that he or she had less money than friends had.

   _____ My fiancé felt that the people around him or her placed too much importance on money.

   _____ My fiancé was embarrassed by being seen as a "rich kid."

_____ My fiancé knew he or she wanted to grow up to have a lot of money.

_____ Other: _____

3. How will these patterns affect your marital relationship?

Study the following passages to discover how to acquire, how to regard, and how to spend money. Indicate the principles that you derive from each passage.

1. Deuteronomy 8:17,18

2. 1 Chronicles 29:11,12

3. Proverbs 11:24,25

4. Proverbs 11:28

5. Proverbs 12:10

6. Proverbs 13:11; 14:23

7. Proverbs 13:18,22

8. Proverbs 15:6

9. Proverbs 15:16,17,22

10. Proverbs 15:27

11. Proverbs 16:8

12. Proverbs 16:16

13. Proverbs 20:4,14,18

14. Proverbs 21:5,6

15. Proverbs 21:20,25,26

16. Proverbs 22:1,4,7

17. Proverbs 23:1-5

18. Proverbs 24:30-34

19. Proverbs 27:23,24

20. Proverbs 28:6,22

21. Proverbs 30:24,25

22. Ecclesiastes 5:10

23. Ecclesiastes 5:19

24. Matthew 6:19,20

25. Matthew 17:24-27

26. Luke 6:27-38

27. Luke 12:13-21

28. Romans 13:6-8

29. Ephesians 4:28

30. Philippians 4:11-19

31. 2 Thessalonians 3:7-12

32. 1 Timothy 6:6-10

33. 1 Timothy 6:17-19

34. Hebrews 13:5

Have you ever wondered how much you are worth?
Let's find out by completing this worksheet. You may be surprised.

What Are You Worth?[28]

ASSETS (at sell value)

Cash (checking, money-market accounts,
    savings, CDs)... $ _____

Invested Assets

    Insurance and Annuities .... _____

    Stocks and Stock Mutual Funds.................................... _____

    Bonds and Bond Mutual Funds.................................... _____

    Partnerships.. _____

    Residence.. _____

    Other Real Estate.. _____

Notes and Trust Deeds. . . . . _____

IRAs and Other Retirement Accounts . . . . _____

Other Assets. . . . . _____

Total Invested Assets $ _____

Personal Assets

Furnishings . . . . _____

Automobiles . . . . _____

Collections . . . . _____

Other. . . . . _____

Total Personal Assets $ _____

TOTAL ASSETS $ _____

LIABILITIES

Secured Liabilities

Mortgage on Residence . . . . _____

Automobile Loans . . . . _____

Notes and Trust Deeds. . . . . _____

Loans Against Life Insurance . . . . _____

Other. . . . . _____

Total Secured Liabilities $ _____

Unsecured Liabilities

Charge Accounts . . . . _____

Bills Due . . . . _____

Personal Loans. . . . . _____

Other. . . . . _____

Total Unsecured Liabilities $ _____

TOTAL ASSETS $ _____

– TOTAL LIABILITIES $ _____

TOTAL NET WORTH $ _____

Dos and Don'ts for Budgeting

1. Plan your budget together. Set a specific time together to review your fiancé's financials and your own. Discuss and create a general budget. Seek agreement and cooperation. Make decisions together. Figures and plans should be known by both of you.

2. Define your general financial goals. Launch your budget with a clear idea of why you're setting a budget.

3. Don't finalize a budget before you both know how much you now spend for what. Devote several weeks to keeping detailed expense records for use in working on a budget. If you do not know where your money is going, you cannot sensibly decide where it should go. Set a date for your next budget meeting.

4. Do not think up countless budget headings. Use common sense in approaching and clarifying and classifying according to your spending habits.

5. Divvy up your dollars according to your united needs and wants. Do not allocate according to the way other people spend. Use averages, online guides, and outside resources as rough starting points only.

Now list your specific needs and wants individually and as a couple.

Needs

Wants

6. Think first. When allocating, trimming, or adjusting budget amounts, do not jump to conclusions. Do not let wishful thinking take the place of sober appraisal. Does an expense item look too high? Find out whether it really is high, or why it is high, before cutting it. If you are looking for a place to economize so you can spend more on something else, do not cut arbitrarily. Before you do whittle down an item, spell out precisely what specific items of past expenditures are to be reduced or eliminated.

7. Take all credit cards—except one for emergencies—out of your wallet. Cancel multiple Visas and MasterCards. Don't let them become a way of financing your daily living.

8. Don't carry your checkbook or debit card around. Write one allowance check every week per person . . . for lunches, newspapers and magazines, groceries, dry cleaning, and laundering. Cash the checks—and don't spend more than that for those expenses during the week. Become your own banker, and learn how to say no.

9. Plan for the big expenses. You can expect several big, nonrecurring expenses during the year—taxes, insurance, vacation bills, etc. Forecast those expenses and put aside an amount each month to meet them when they come due. If not planned for, a few of these expenses will throw your budget into chaos, from which it may never recover.

10. Know who is in charge of what. Each person should know just what his or her responsibilities are.

11. Experiment. For two months, each of you write down every penny you spend. When you buy a candy bar from the vending machine at work, write it down. When you write your mortgage check, note it in the book. At the end of each of the two months, review your expenses and label them "O" for optional and "E" for essential. The challenge is to eliminate the optional expenses that give you the least value for your money.

12. Except for the above experiment, do not keep track of every penny. Each person should be allowed to spend an allowance as he or she chooses without having to make an entry in the budget. Do not insist that everyone keep itemized lists of all expenses. Do not demand detailed accounts and summaries.

13. Do not intermingle funds. Keep separate accounts for monthly spending and savings. Have a clear-cut system for divvying up the paychecks. A checking account is a good system. You deposit a sum of money each payday to cover expenses, keeping a record of how much is earmarked for what. This way you will not be spending more than you have allotted for any one budget item.

14. Do not cheat your budget. For example, if your budget shows you cannot afford a new ski outfit this month, do not go out and

charge it. A debt like this should always be taken into account for next month's planning. Otherwise, you will find that a substantial amount of your funds has already been spent because of interest.

15. Use automatic deduction. No matter how strapped for cash you feel you are, authorize automatic deductions from your salary for 401(k) savings and retirement programs.

16. Don't carry around too much cash—you will tend to spend it. Go to ATMs only as planned, not to pocket an extra $100. If you face an emergency, fine. But don't run to the machine or use smart technology just to buy an unbudgeted item on sale.

17. Avoid shopping retail. There's no reason to pay an outrageous markup on retail items when outlet shops and online sources offer tremendous discounts.

18. When the budget starts to rub tight, let it out here, tuck it in there, to give a better fit. Do not keep it ironclad and inflexible. A grim, unbending budget will soon make everybody sullen, if not outright mutinous. A good rule of evaluation is to look at your budget every January and every July to make certain that it is realistic and working for your benefit.

And do not quit your budget at the first bump. Budgets seldom click the first time around. Hang on, start revising, try fresh ideas. Do not toss in the towel. If at first you don't succeed, you know what to do![29]

As you make out your budget, be sure to insert an item designated "Marriage Enrichment." This amount, which could be from $50 to $250 per year, is for the enhancement of your marriage relationship. It can be used for books to read together, seminars to listen to or watch or attend, romantic weekends, marriage retreats, etc. By doing this and planning this as a goal, you can build the quality of married life that you are both seeking. It doesn't just happen! It takes planning and effort.

How will the presence of Jesus Christ in your life help you with the financial aspects of your life together?"

Resources About Personal Finance

8 Important Money Decisions for Every Couple and *The Truth About Money Lies.* Both are by Russ Crosson, president of Ronald Blue & Co., a Christian-based, full-service, well-respected financial planning and investment management firm.

CHAPTER 12

Sex in Marriage

✿

The Bible talks about four specific purposes for human sexual activity: procreation, recreation, communication, and release. Look into what God's Word says about each of these purposes by reading the following Bible verses and talking over the discussion questions.

Procreation. Read Genesis 1:28 and Deuteronomy 7:13,14. What evidence do these verses give that sexual activity for reproduction of the human race is part of God's design?

Read Psalm 127:3 and Psalm 139:13-15 from The Living Bible. What attitude toward human sexuality and reproduction do you discover in these verses?

Recreation and Release. Read Song of Solomon 4:10-12 and Proverbs 5:18,19. Does it surprise or shock you that the Scriptures encourage the enjoyment and sensual delights of sex?

Reread Proverbs 5:18,19, remembering that the writer used poetic language as he spoke of sexual energies, drives, and outlets. Throughout the Bible a favorite symbol for sex is *water*—fountains, streams, cisterns, springs, wells, etc. Do you agree or disagree that Proverbs 5:18,19 encourages a husband and a wife to come to their bed to experience sexual pleasure? Write reasons why you agree or disagree.

Communication. Read Genesis 2:24. Ideally, the "one flesh" spoken of in this verse means a blending of spirit, mind, soul—your entire being—with your spouse. Read the following paragraph that more fully describes the concept of "one flesh." Then answer the questions.

In the plan of God, sex was intended to provide a means of totally revealing oneself to the beloved, of pouring one's energies and deepest affection, hopes, and dreams into the loved one. Sex provides a means of presenting one's spouse with the gift of oneself and experiencing a like gift in return—a means of saying "I love you." In short, sex becomes a mode of communication, a means of knowing each other.

How do everyday experiences affect sexual closeness and communication? How can they affect a husband's or a wife's ability to give of oneself to the other?

1. What was the first question about sex that you can remember asking your parents? How did they respond?

2. From what source (parents, friends, media, websites, books) did you first learn the basic facts (or rumors) about reproduction? Can you remember anything about how you felt when you received this information?

3. When you were growing up, did you have anyone with whom you felt comfortable asking questions concerning sex? Who was it? What made that person easy to talk with?

4. The word sex means . . .

5. In marriage, sex is . . .

6. What are two descriptions that characterize your feelings about sex?

7. Describe how you feel about your body.

8. What are your needs for physical affection?

9. Describe any concerns or fears you have concerning sex.

10. Describe your level of comfort when you touch and are touched.

11. What events and attitudes from your past have influenced your sexual behaviors and attitudes? What have you shared with your fiancé? Is there anything you're hesitant to share?

12. What do you look forward to sexually in your marriage?

13. What worries you about sex in your upcoming marriage?

14. Do you find any specific sexual acts immoral (improper) in marriage? Do you have any hesitations or reservations about sex?

15. As a sexual partner, a wife should . . .

16. As a sexual partner, a husband should . . .

17. Agree or disagree: Men are "women watchers"; women are not normally "men watchers."

18. After you are married, how will you respond and deal with another person being attracted to you and approaching you?

19. What will you do if you find yourself attracted to another person?

20. On a scale of 0 to 10, how important is sex in a Christian couple's marriage?

0	5	10

21. What difference will being Christians make in a couple's sexual relationship in marriage?[30]

Together, read this prayer written by Harry Hollis, Jr., and then discuss how you feel about the content.

Lord, it's hard to know what sex really is—
Is it some demon put here to torment me?
Or some delicious seducer from reality?
It is neither of these, Lord.
I know what sex is—
It is body and spirit,
It is passion and tenderness,
It is strong embrace and gentle hand-holding,

It is open nakedness and hidden mystery,
It is joyful tears on honeymoon faces, and
It is tears on wrinkled faces at a golden wedding
    anniversary.
Sex is a quiet look across the room,
    A love note on a pillow,
    A rose laid on a breakfast plate,
    Laughter in the night.
Sex is life—not all of life—
    But wrapped up in the meaning of life.
Sex is your good gift, O God,
    To enrich life,
    To continue the race,
    To communicate,
    To show me who I am,
    To reveal my mate,
    To cleanse through "one flesh."
Lord, some people say
    Sex and religion don't mix;
But your Word says sex is good.
Help me to keep it good in my life.
Help me to be open about sex
    And still protect its mystery.
    Help me to see that sex
    Is neither demon nor deity.
Help me not climb into a fantasy world
    Of imaginary sexual partners;
Keep me in the real world
    To love the people you have created.
Teach me that my soul does not have to frown
    at sex
    For me to be a Christian.
    It's hard for many people to say,
    "Thank God for sex!"
Because for them sex is more a problem
    Than a gift.
They need to know that sex and gospel
Can be linked together again.
They need to hear the good news about sex.

Show me how I can help them.
Thank you, Lord, for making me a sexual being.
Thank you for showing me how to treat others
    with trust and love.
Thank you for letting me talk to you about sex.
Thank you that I feel free to say:
    "Thank God for sex!"[31]

The material in this section on sexuality is simply an introduction. It is very important that you be fully informed of both the physiological and biblical facts concerning sex. The vast majority of individuals are not nearly as informed as they could be. Women are more informed in most cases than men.

Prior to your marriage, we highly recommend that you read *Intended for Pleasure* by Dr. Ed Wheat, a Christian medical doctor, and Gaye Wheat. In addition, the book *The Gift of Sex* by Cliff and Joyce Penner is an excellent presentation. Both of these books can be ordered online or by telephone at Christian Marriage Enrichment, 800-875-7560, www.hnormanwright.com.

CHAPTER 13

Your Spiritual Life Together

✧

Spiritual intimacy. What's that? Spiritual intimacy is a heart desire to be close to God and submit to His direction for your lives. It is the willingness to seek His guidance together and to allow the teaching of His Word in your everyday life. It's a willingness to allow God to help you overcome any discomfort over sharing spiritually and learning to see your coming marriage as a spiritual adventure. It's a willingness to enthrone Jesus Christ as Lord of your lives and to look to Him for direction in your decisions, including which house to buy, where to go on vacations, and which school is best for the children. It means He will direct both of you and change your hearts to be in agreement rather than speak through just one of you.

Lordship and Control

Spiritual intimacy in marriage requires both partners to submit to the leadership and lordship of Christ instead of competing for control. One author wrote:

We can gather all facts needed in making a decision. We can thresh out our differences as to the shape and direction our decision should take. We can put off the decision while we allow the relevant information to simmer in our minds. Even then, however, we may be uneasy; we still don't know what is best to do, and the right decision just won't come.

When we turn to the Lord Jesus Christ and open our consciences to His Spirit's leading, some new events, remembrances, and forgotten facts will come to us. A whole new pattern will emerge. We can then move with abandon in a whole new direction which we had not previously considered. Looking back, we may conclude that God's providence delivered us from what would have been the worst possible decision. Jesus as Lord made the difference between deliverance and destruction.[32]

For a couple to have spiritual intimacy, they need shared beliefs as to who Jesus is and the basic tenets of the Christian faith. You may have different beliefs about the second coming of Christ or whether all the spiritual gifts are for today. One of you may enjoy an informal church service while the other likes a formal service. One of you may be charismatic and the other not. There can still be spiritual intimacy within this diversity.

We hear about mismatched couples—when one is a Christian and one isn't. You can also have a mismatch when both are believers: One wants to grow and is growing, but the other doesn't and isn't.[33]

A wonderful way to encourage spiritual intimacy is to share the history of your spiritual life. Many couples know where their partners are currently but have very little knowledge of how they came to that place.

Use the following questions to discover more about your partner's faith.

1. What did your parents believe about God, Jesus, church, prayer, and the Bible?

2. What is your definition of being "spiritually alive"?

3. Which parent did you see as being more spiritually alive?

4. What specifically did each parent teach you, directly and indirectly, about spiritual matters?

5. Where did you first learn about God? About Jesus? About the Holy Spirit? At what age?

6. What was your best experience in church as a child? As a teen?

7. What was your worst experience in church as a child? As a teen?

8. Describe your conversion experience. When was it? Who was involved? Where did it take place?

9. Describe your baptism. What does it mean to you?

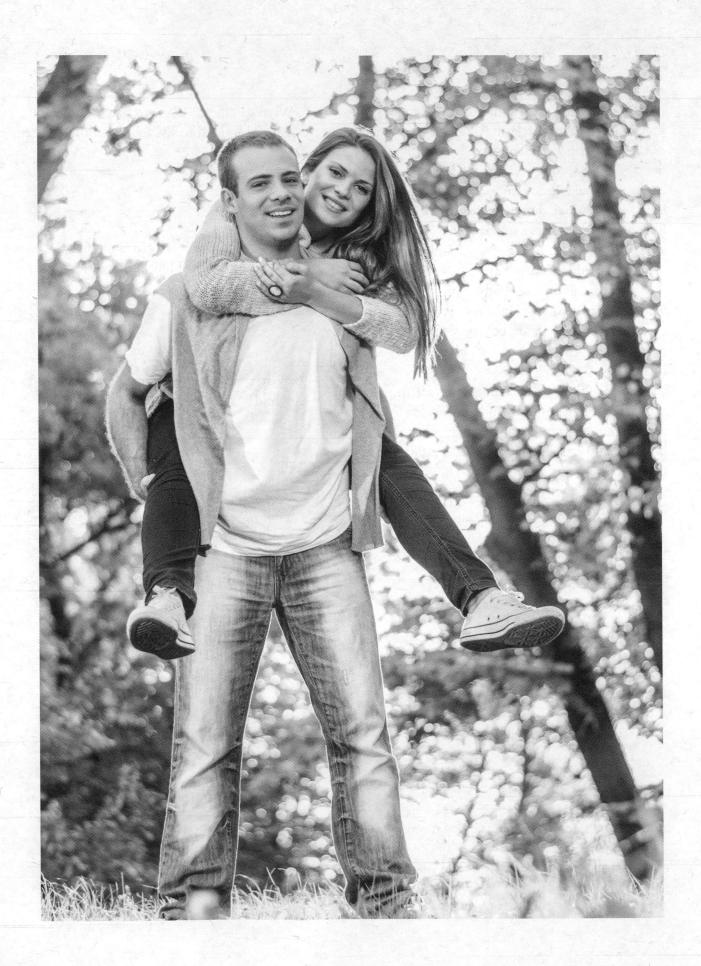

10. Which Sunday school teacher influenced you the most? In what way?

11. Which minister influenced you the most? In what way?

12. What questions did you have as a child/teen about your faith? Who gave you answers?

13. Was there any camp or special meeting that affected you spiritually?

14. Did you read the Bible as a teen?

15. Did you memorize any Scripture as a child or teen? Do you remember any now?

16. As a child, if you could have asked God any questions, what would they have been?

17. As a teen, if you could have asked God any questions, what would they have been?

18. If you could ask God any questions now, what would they be?

19. What would have helped you spiritually when you were growing up?

20. Did anyone disappoint you spiritually as a child? If so, how has that impacted you as an adult?

21. When you went through difficult times as a child or teen, how did that affect your faith?

22. What has been the greatest spiritual experience of your life?

23. When you pray, what do you pray about?

24. After the wedding, do you want to pray together? If so, how often? Do you want to read a devotional together or separately? How frequently do you want to attend church? How do you see you and your spouse serving Christ together?

You may want to begin sharing God's Word and devotions together at this time. *Quiet Times for Couples* provides daily readings for couples, and when children come along *Quiet Times for Parents* provides parenting encouragement and advice through insightful devotions. These are authored by H. Norman Wright and available online or by telephone at Christian Marriage Enrichment, 800-875-7560, www.hnormanwright.com.

Planning Your Wedding Together

❧

Getting married is a giant step. So is planning the wedding. This ought to be a time of enjoyment, delight, fun, laughter, and a drawing together of family members. Too often it isn't. Conflicts can occur between the prospective bride and groom and/or the couple and their parents. Keep in mind that whatever could go wrong on your wedding day may actually happen. So go to your wedding with this attitude: Something will probably go wrong, and that's all right. We can handle it. It won't be the end of the world. If something does go awry, we'll just fix it and go on to plan B. We can handle it. We'll end up with an unplanned memory from our wedding day. Above all, have a sense of humor and a sense of acceptance.

To help you with your wedding plans, complete and discuss the following:

1. What I want for our wedding is . . .

2. What my fiancé wants for our wedding is . . .

3. What my mother wants for our wedding is . . .

4. What my father wants for our wedding is . . .

5. Our wedding will take place at . . .

6. The reason this location was selected was...

7. The person most involved in planning this wedding is . . .

8. The way I feel about this is . . .

9. What I wish could be changed about our planned wedding is . . .

10. I wish my fiancé would be *more / less* involved in the planning of our wedding.

11. The person most uptight about our wedding is _____ and the reason is . . .

12. The person we are having the greatest difficulty with while planning our wedding is . . .

13. The way in which I would like the people attending our wedding to participate is . . .

14. The way in which I would like the people attending our wedding to remember and be impacted by our wedding is . . .

15. The way in which I would like Jesus Christ represented and glorified in our wedding is . . .

A Marriage Benediction

May your marriage bring you all the fulfillment a marriage should bring, and may the Lord give you patience, tolerance, and understanding. May it be full of joy and laughter, as well as comfort and support. May you discover the true depth of love through loving one another.

Remember that every burden is easier to carry when you have the shoulders of two instead of one. When you are weary and discouraged, look to Jesus to refresh and strengthen you.

May you always need one another—not so much to fill your emptiness, but to help you know your fullness. May you always need one another, but not out of weakness. Rejoice in and praise one another's uniqueness, for God is the Creator of both male and female and differences in personality.

Be faithful to one another in your thoughts and deeds, and above all, be faithful to Jesus. May you see the marriage bed as an altar of grace and pleasure. May you remember that each time you speak to one another you are talking to someone that God has claimed and considers very special. View and treat your partner as one created in the image of God. Remember that you are not to hold your mate captive, but to give your new spouse the freedom to become all that God wants. May you embrace and hold one another, but not encircle one another.

May God renew your minds so you draw out the best and the potential in one another. Look for things to praise, never take one another for granted, often say "I love you," and take no notice of little faults. Affirm one another, defer to one another, and believe in your partner. If you have differences that push you apart, may both of you have the good sense to take the first step back. May the phrases "You're right," "Forgive me," and "I forgive you" be close at hand.

Thank You, heavenly Father, for Your presence here with us and for Your blessing upon this marriage.

In Jesus' name, amen.

NOTES

1. Sydney Smith, *Lady Holland's Memoir*, Vol. I (London: Longman, Brown, Green & Longman, 1855).

2. David Augsburger, *Cherishable: Love and Marriage* (Scottdale, PA: Herald Press, 1971), p. 16.

3. D. Elton Trueblood.

4. Daniel Freeman, "Why Get Married?" *Theology News and Notes of Fuller Theological Seminary*, 1973 (December 1973, 19:4), p. 17.

5. From a message by Dr. David Hubbard, president of Fuller Theological Seminary.

6. David Augsburger, *Sustaining Love* (Ventura, CA: Regal Books, 1988), p. 40.

7. Ira J. Tanner, *Loneliness: The Fear of Love* (New York: Harper & Row, 1973), pp. 92, 93, adapted.

8. H. Norman Wright, *Secrets of a Lasting Marriage* (Ventura, CA: Regal Books, 1995), p. 128, adapted.

9. Abraham Schmitt, *Conflict and Ecstasy—Model for a Maturing Marriage*, an original paper.

10. James G.T. Fairfield, *When You Don't Agree: A Guide to Resolving Marriage and Family Conflict* (Scottdale, PA: Herald Press, 1977), p. 195.

11. Augsburger, *Sustaining Love*, pp. 54-56.

12. Mel Krantzer, *Creative Marriage* (New York: McGraw Hill, 1988), p. 54, adapted.

13. Paul Welter, *Family Problems and Predicaments* (Wheaton, IL: Tyndale House, 1977), p. 101.

14. George Barna, *The Power of Vision* (Ventura, CA: Regal Books, 1992), pp. 28-28, adapted.

15. Ibid., pp. 98-99, adapted.

16. Wright, *Secrets of a Lasting Marriage*, p. 72.

17. Ibid., p. 75, adapted.

18. Dwight H. Small, *Christian: Celebrate Your Sexuality* (Old Tappan, NJ: Revell, 1974), p. 144.

19. Dennis Guernsey, *Thoroughly Married* (Waco, TX: Word Books, 1976), p. 70.

20. James Olthuis, *I Pledge Thee My Troth* (New York: Harper & Row, 1975), p. 27.

21. Reuel Howe, *Herein Is Love* (Valley Forge, PA: Judson Press, 1961), p. 100.

22. David and Vera Mace, *We Can Have Better Marriages If We Really Want Them* (Nashville: Abingdon Press, 1974).

23. Albert Metowbian, *Silent Messages* (Belmont, CA: Wadsworth Publishing Company, 1971), pp. 42-44.

24. Adapted from John Powell, *Why Am I Afraid to Tell You Who I Am?* (Niles, IL: Argus Communications, 1969), pp. 54-62.

25. Ross Campbell, *How to Really Love Your Child* (Wheaton, IL: Victor Books, 1977), p. 20.

26. Paul Tournier, *To Understand Each Other* (Richmond, VA: John Knox Press, 1967), p. 29.

27. James Fairfield, *When You Don't Agree* (Herald Press), pp. 33, 34, 231.

28. Busby, Barber & Temple, *The Christian's Guide to Worry-Free Money Management* (Grand Rapids, MI: Zondervan, 1994), adapted.

29. Some questions taken from: Busby, Barber & Temple, *The Christian's Guide*.

30. Some questions taken from or adapted from: *Preparing for Marriage* (Augsburg Fortress, 1992).

31. Harry Hollis, Jr., *Thank God for Sex* (Nashville: Broadman Press, 1975), pp. 11-12.

32. Howard and Jeanne Hendricks, general editors, with LaVonne Neff, *Husbands and Wives* (Wheaton, IL: Victor Books, 1988), p. 158.

33. Donald R. Harvey, *The Spiritually Intimate Marriage* (Grand Rapids, MI: Fleming H. Revell, 1991), p. 24.

PERSONAL NOTES

PERSONAL NOTES

PERSONAL NOTES

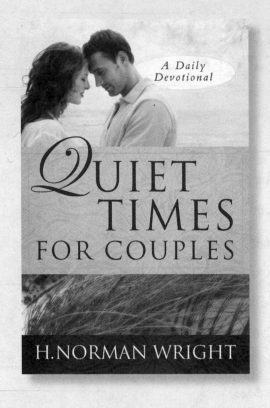

Quiet Times for Couples

by H. Norman Wright

**Uplifting, insightful devotions
that will inspire, encourage, and
strengthen your marriage**

In these short devotions that promote togetherness, joy, and sharing your dreams,
trusted Christian counselor and bestselling author Norm Wright offers…

- innovative ideas to establish and maintain a flourishing marriage

- insights for encouraging intimacy and harmony

- little and big things you can do to enhance your relationship

- specific suggestions for accommodating differences and handling conflicts

- great ideas for supporting and helping your spouse

Your relationship will become more loving, considerate, and united as the two
of you experience these quiet "together times" filled with deep insights, powerful
meditations, God's presence, and His truths and love.

*"Let Norman Wright guide you together to God…
and your marriage will never be the same."*

Max Lucado